WILLIAM
the rebel prince

WILLIAM
the rebel prince

NICHOLAS DAVIES

PICTURES BY
MARK SAUNDERS

JOHN BLAKE

Published by John Blake Ltd,
3 Bramber Court, 2 Bramber Road,
London W14 9PB, England

First published in paperback in 2001
ISBN 1 903402 28 X

British Library Cataloguing-in-Publication Data:

A catalogue record for this book is
available from the British Library.

Typeset by Jon Davies

Printed in Great Britain by
Creative Print and Design (Wales),
Ebbw Vale, Gwent.

1 3 5 7 9 10 8 6 4 2

Contents

This book is dedicated to Thomas

*Grateful acknowledgements
go to my friends in Royal households
who have been so kind in helping me
put together this book.
For obvious reasons they cannot be named.*

Part One

The Rebel

1

Crown and Country

After many months of deliberation, Prince William has informed his father that he wants to drop the title of 'Prince' and continue the tradition he initiated some years ago of being called simply by his first name, William. Throughout his years at both Ludgrove and Eton, it was simply William's Christian name that everyone used.

Far more importantly, however, William has also told his father that he does not wish to remain heir to the throne and wants to renounce formally all claim to the throne.

In numerous conversations with Prince Charles, William has insisted that his rejection of his title and his claim to the Crown is no teenage rebellion, something that will pass with time, but a decision that he has been mulling over for a couple of years.

In straight-talking discussions, William has insisted, 'I don't want to be King, I don't want the job.'

William first had a conversation along these lines with his father in the autumn of 2000. Understandably, Charles was deeply concerned, realising full well that if William did indeed go through with his intentions, his decision would create the most enormous constitutional crisis. Such a dramatic and far reaching decision would, most likely, have disastrous consequences for both the House of Windsor and, perhaps, for the very survival of the hereditary monarchy in Britain.

If William persists with his refusal to accept his hereditary right to the Crown, the repercussions of such a decision will be the most serious the monarchy has faced since

1937 when Edward VIII took his historic decision to abdicate so that he could marry the woman he loved, the American divorcee Wallis Simpson.

Prince Charles, however, remains confident that William's opposition and discontent with the role he has been destined to fulfil in life is only a youthful flickering of disloyal rebellion which will pass with time.

Nonetheless, Charles finally decided to inform the Queen of his conversations with William, and seek her advice. The news of William's negative attitude to the monarchy and his unwillingness to take seriously his responsibility to the Royal Family horrified her.

The Queen's first reaction was to instruct Charles to 'get a grip' of his wayward son and instill in him the meaning of the word 'duty'. She told Charles to pass on her message to William, telling him in no uncertain terms that there could be no rejection of his role of heir to the throne and that he should banish all such thoughts from his mind.

She instructed Charles to inform William

that his role in life had been pre-determined by the accident of birth. He had been born into the Royal Family — a hereditary monarchy — and, as the eldest child of Prince Charles, he is heir to the throne and nothing will change that state of affairs.

Indeed, the Queen then turned on Charles, blaming him for not bringing up William to understand that he has never had a choice as to whether he does or doesn't want to be King. He was born to be King and, as far as the Queen is concerned, nothing that William has said has changed that fact. Nor will it.

Privately, however, senior courtiers confirm that the Queen is deeply worried by William's desire to abdicate his responsibilities to his father, to the Royal House of Windsor and to the throne.

William had further conversations with Charles on his return from Patagonia at the end of 2000 and again in the summer of 2001, when he returned from his four-month safari in Southern Africa. During these conversations, however, William has continued to reiterate his stance that he wants no future as a prince of the realm, heir to the throne, and certainly not as the future monarch.

Throughout his gap year, William should have been attending a series of tutorials with constitutional lawyers and senior royal aides responsible for educating him about the role of the monarchy within the British Constitution. Their duty was to explain the minutiae of Britain's unwritten Constitution; the relationship between the monarchy and the government; and the disciplines within which the monarch must remain when dealing with the Prime Minister, affairs of State or when meeting foreign dignitaries.

In his time, Prince Charles had to attend such tutorials, which continued while he was at Cambridge University. But William has hardly attended any tutorials throughout his gap year.

Indeed, William told a friend of his from his Eton days, 'I'm in deep trouble ... it's HM ... you know that I'm meant to study all this constitutional stuff about the monarchy and how it works ... well, basically, I haven't done it, I haven't done anything actually.'

He also confided that Prince Charles would also be in hot water because he hadn't made sure that William attended the tutorials or read the books. William said, 'HM gave him a ticking-off because he should have made sure that I did the work, you know, reading volumes of books, boring stuff that no one is interested in. My father had to study it when he was my age. He agrees it's boring stuff but it goes with the job.'

The Queen discussed the issue with her most senior advisers and came to the conclusion that she had to take some action in an effort to dissuade William from going through with his threat to renounce the throne.

After these consultations, the Queen came to the conclusion that the senior aides in Prince Charles' office were not proving effective enough in guiding and influencing Charles or strong enough to enforce the rigid disciplines of the family towards the monarchy and the House of Windsor.

That was the primary reason why the

Queen has signalled that Sir Michael Charles Gerard Peat KCVO, Keeper of the Privy Purse and Treasurer to the Queen, one of her most senior and trusted aides, should take over from Prince Charles' Secretary Stephen Lamport when he retires in the summer of 2002.

Educated at Eton and Trinity College, Oxford, Sir Michael, now 51, trained as an accountant and joined the international accountancy firm KPMG Peat Marwick, where members of his family had also worked. In 1990, he was appointed Director of Finance and Property Services of Her Majesty's Household before gaining promotion to his present powerful job in 1994.

A married man with two sons and two daughters, Sir Michael is seen as a quiet, bookish type of person with a strong sense of duty and views of the monarchy similar to those of the Queen. The Queen believes that Sir Michael will be the man to add backbone to Prince Charles' office. His job will not only entail advising Charles on all principal matters, but he will also keep a close eye on both the wayward young William and the fun-loving, cheeky Harry who is also showing signs of teenage rebellion.

Prince Charles had been grooming his deputy secretary Mark Bolland to take over the top job from Stephen Lamport but the Queen was of the belief that Mark Bolland's influence is too trendy, too modern and not of sufficient discipline and dedication to the onerous task of private secretary to the Prince of Wales. Friends of Mark Bolland report that he has been deeply hurt at being passed over for the top job. Other friends say that he became angry and upset when he first heard that Sir Michael Peat had been given the job that he had coveted for so long.

Charles prefers to take a much less heavy-handed approach to the whole affair, still hoping that William can be persuaded to accept his lot in life and understand that, despite his objections, he has no real choice. Charles believes that young William will not react favourably to strong-arm tactics and bullying. As a result, Prince Charles continues to discuss the matter with William, arguing that the monarchy is all about duty and responsibility and is hopeful that, in time, William will come to understand that and bend to the will of his father and the Queen.

Prince Charles also tried another tactic. It was some time after William's initial shock revelation to his father that Charles hit upon the idea of asking his former equerry, Captain Mark Dyer, a burly, red-haired former Welsh Guards officer, to accompany young William on his world travels during his gap year.

William had always respected Mark Dyer and they had become quite close during the time Dyer was dating Tiggy Legge-Bourke in the early 1990s. Since those times, Mark has been an occasional visitor to Highgrove during school holidays and William has always felt he could speak openly and honestly to the older man. Indeed, Mark once described himself as William's 'companion and mentor'.

Prince Charles called Mark in for a chat some time after he had accompanied William to Belize on a two-week jungle survival course with the Welsh Guards. Charles asked him if he could take time off to accompany William both to Mauritius, on a scientific and ecological research programme run by the Royal Geographical Society, and to Patagonia, where William was to spend ten weeks teaching English as a Raleigh International volunteer.

It was following these trips that Charles took Dyer into his confidence and told him of William's denial of his whole future as a member of the Royal Family and his wish to relinquish his right to the throne. Charles asked whether it would be possible for him to accompany William to Africa for four months so that he could visit Kenya and Botswana on safari — hunting, tracking and shooting game.

More importantly, Charles asked him if, during their months together, he could talk man-to-man with William about the monarchy, his responsibilities to the family and his duty to the nation. Mark agreed to talk to him and see what he could do. Charles had confidence that Mark might be just the person to persuade William to toe the royal line.

Prince Charles hoped that Dyer could fill the role for William that Charles' guru, Sir

Laurens van der Post — philosopher-poet, explorer and author — undertook, influencing Charles' outlook on life during their two-month tour of the southern African continent some 30 years earlier.

To his many army friends, Mark has always been known as 'straight down the line and down-to-earth, with an easy-going sense of humour; a man who doesn't stand on ceremony'. William likes that about him.

The safaris went fantastically well, with William describing his adventures in Botswana as 'wicked'. Mark Dyer returned to London some weeks before William and reported to Prince Charles that he had spoken at length to William about his future and his duty to the Royal Family. But Mark had found William adamant that he did not want to continue in his present role as a prince and heir to the throne, but William did agree 'to think about it'.

Following his return from Botswana, Prince Charles also asked William whether he would be happy to take part in the celebrations planned for the Queen's Golden Jubilee in 2002. It had always been hoped and expected that both William and Harry would play a significant role and make several appearances across the country.

Some of the Queen's most senior advisers believe that Prince William's ability, in particular, to capture the public imagination could be the key to a successful year of festivities. They were convinced that William's presence at the side of the Queen at a number of public engagements would fire the enthusiasm of the nation, particularly among young people. Without William's presence, they feared the celebrations might flop.

The Queen's senior aides, tasked with the planning of the Golden Jubilee celebrations, had written in both William and Harry to play prominent roles. One commented, 'We hope and expect Prince William will play a big role.'

In the Spring of 2001, a secret Mori Poll —commissioned by the Way Ahead Group, consisting of senior members of the Royal

Family and senior aides — revealed that fewer than half of the population thought the Royal Family to be 'important to Britain'. Fewer than one in four considered that they were hard-working, and only one in ten believed that they were value for money.

However, in a dramatic gesture of open defiance, William told his father that he wants nothing to do with the Golden Jubilee celebrations. He doesn't want to tour the country making appearances with the Queen because that would show the nation that he was happy with his role as heir to the throne, a prince of the realm. Once again, he emphasised to Prince Charles that he is determined to keep out of the limelight as much as possible because he has no wish to continue in the role destiny has forced upon him.

As a result, William has refused to take part in all but one of the many celebrations and his single appearance is expected to be on the one occasion when the entire Royal Family will gather in June of 2002 to celebrate the Jubilee.

William's refusal caused a furious row between Prince Charles and the Queen and Prince Philip, who both believed that Charles should order William to take part in the celebrations. But Charles stood firm, believing that bullying William would have no effect and might even make him more rebellious.

In an effort to conceal the true situation of William's defiance, Prince Charles let it be known that he, personally, has taken the decision not to permit William to take part in the celebrations so that his son can concentrate on his studies at St Andrew's.

There are those close to Prince Charles who believe that William is acting out in his own life what he had learned from his beloved mother when he would listen to her launching into anti-monarchist diatribes about the Royal Family, the Queen and, particularly, Prince Philip. There are others who believe that William is 'a chip off the old block' and that, in his heart, he feels the same way towards the Royal Family and the monarchy as his mother did.

Princess Diana was unable to accept the

tough disciplines of life within the Royal Family and needed to escape from the strict confines and rigid rules of 'the Firm'. Headstrong and determined, Diana finally did break away and began to lead her own life. In doing so, Diana won the love and devotion of the nation and the respect of people around the world. William may simply be following in her footsteps.

Whatever happens, Prince William will have his wish of being known simply as plain 'William' throughout the next three years at St Andrew's University in Scotland where he will be studying History of Art. He will also have those years to think through his future as a member of the Royal Family, heir to the throne, prince of the realm.

2

A Year of Action

William has really enjoyed his year of freedom. No school, no classes, no university, no tutorials and no exams. For the first time in his life, he felt a freedom that he had never before experienced. With no responsibilities and no disciplines, he could do whatever he wished, within reason.

The young prince was in his element. In the final months of 2000, he awoke early most mornings and, after showering, would dress for a day of the sport he adores above all others — shooting.

As an eighteenth birthday present, William was given a 12-bore Purdey shotgun by his father, his first custom-built sporting gun. It is his pride and joy. During that first winter of glorious independence, William let his friends, and his father's friends, know that he was as keen as mustard to attend as many shoots as possible right up to the end of the game-shooting season on 31 January. He told them that he would be happy to drive to Scotland, the North of England or, indeed, anywhere in Britain for the chance of honing his skills in the field.

As a result, the invitations came thick and fast, particularly from two of Prince Charles's close friends, the Duke of Westminster and Lord Soames, both of whom are keen shots. Even when there were no shooting parties, William would occasionally shoot with his father and his friends. They might shoot near Highgrove, at Sandringham or drive to Gerald Grosvenor's 14,000-acre shooting estate at Abbeystead, north of Preston.

William has taken to shooting with tremendous enthusiasm despite the fact that Princess Diana had done her utmost to persuade her first-born that shooting was cruel, a sport that he should never indulge in.

Diana would put to a young William the alternative view, that shooting birds, deer or rabbits was a cruel act, explaining that no one should kill for pleasure. William and Harry were left in no doubt as to their mother's dislike, even loathing, for the sport. Throughout their childhood, she had tried to dissuade them from joining the Royal Family shoots by planning other adventures, other pursuits and encouraging other interests. Later, Diana would explain to her sons that shooting any wild animal or bird was outrageous and bloodthirsty and would urge them to think of the animals. But from the start, Diana was fighting a losing battle.

William loved going out on shoots with his father. He liked the noise of the guns, the excitement of the shoot and the frenetic enthusiasm of the gun dogs. He loved collecting the fallen birds and taking them back for the count. The sense of fun, of excitement, of being involved in an adult sport, thoroughly appealed to him. Diana didn't really stand a chance. She could not and did not win.

Before they were ten years of age, both William and Harry were pleading with their father to allow them to join the family shoots at Balmoral and Sandringham. As he grew older, William would race down to breakfast and tuck into the traditional shooting-party breakfast of porridge followed by kedgeree. He would then rush outside, dressed for the shoot, waiting for the other members of the party to arrive. Come rain or shine, snow or sleet, William would then spend most of the day walking by the side of his father's loader, watching with admiration as his father fired away, usually very successfully.

William also loved watching the dogs being worked with the guns and he learned to appreciate their discipline and their enthusiasm for the sport, as the labradors and springer spaniels picked up each fallen grouse, pheasant or partridge with gentleness, obediently bringing the bird back to the collection point.

On those earlier shooting trips, the Queen and Prince Philip, often accompanied by guests and other members of the family who were staying with the royals, would also go out, meet up with the shooting party at a pre-arranged spot and enjoy a luxurious picnic lunch served by butlers and footmen. On those occasions, Diana would make known her disapproval by remaining alone inside the castle, not wishing to join the rest of the family either at the shoot or even at the famous picnic lunches.

In his innocence, young William would try to persuade his mother to join the party, and to join him in following the guns.

'It's really great, you would love it,' William would say, trying to persuade his mother to share his enthusiasm. On a couple of occasions, Diana did sometimes succumb to William's pleas and went out on shoots but she wasn't happy — she simply could not understand how people could spend hours shooting beautiful innocent creatures like birds or deer just for sport, just for fun.

Famously, Diana had once had an angry exchange with the Queen during a dinner at Balmoral, something that no one before had ever dared to do. On that occasion, Diana had lost her temper and had the temerity to leave the table and storm out of the dining room in tears, an unprecedented act which surprised and shocked everyone at the dinner. No one walks out on the Queen — ever. But Diana did and the Queen took no action. She was more concerned that Diana had become distressed and emotional.

Eventually, a sad Diana came to the conclusion that she could not and would not stop her sons joining the shooting parties so she made her protest by staying away; she preferred to stick to her principles and spend the day inside.

But each and every Christmas holiday, William became more drawn to the sport. When he was permitted to join the shoot at the age of 12 — after being taught to use a light 28-bore shotgun — his interest rocketed. Charles was delighted, and Diana was upset and angry with Charles for encouraging William to take part in what she described as a 'vile, cowardly and shameful' sport.

At Eton, of course, William had thoroughly enjoyed many other sports, but he always looked forward to those days from August until the end of January when he could join shooting parties. By the winter of 2000–01, however, shooting had become William's passion and his favourite sport.

He drove the length and breadth of Britain attending shooting parties. He became a skilled shot. William discovered that he had a good eye and a steady aim and he would often succeed in achieving the largest bag at the end of a day's sport. He principally shot pheasant but he occasionally enjoyed a duck shoot though for that he would use non-lead bismuth cartridges.

But more than anything, he enjoyed the thrill and the challenge of deer shoots at Balmoral when the game-keepers were culling older members of the herds which roam far and wide in that area of Scotland. He understood that culling has to take place each year to keep the herds in top condition and keep down the numbers to protect the crops, gorse and shrubs. William would go out on foot with the game-keepers, stalking the deer for hours at a time armed with binoculars to make sure the deer being targeted were the older members of the herd. He would often walk ten or more miles a day following the herds across the hilly country. On occasions, William was permitted to take out a couple of bucks, and for that he used a bolt-action .243 rifle.

He would return to the castle at dusk and, after a long hot bath and a couple of beers, he would enjoy a good dinner and be in bed early so that he would be fit for the next day's shoot.

He spent the spring of 2001 indulging himself with his two other favourite sports, riding and fishing; once again, two sports his mother never *really* enjoyed, although she didn't disapprove of them.

In between his return from Patagonia and his four month trip to southern Africa, William would occasionally join hunts in various parts of the country but he isn't that keen on chasing foxes around the countryside. It's not that he disapproves of fox hunting in principle, but he finds many of the hunts too crowded, the riding too restrictive and not as exciting or challenging as he would like.

'There's usually too much waiting around,' he would say. 'Hunting can get awfully boring when you're just sitting on a horse and waiting for something to happen. It's fantastic when you're in the middle of a real chase, with the hounds speaking and everyone is riding really fast but that doesn't seem to happen too often. Well, not when I'm out.'

William prefers to go out riding with Harry when his brother is down from Eton, otherwise he invites a couple of former school friends from Eton, who are also enjoying a gap year. Sometimes, they will all go out for a really good hard ride around Highgrove, Windsor or Sandringham and tackle an event course which he finds difficult, demanding and really exciting. The tougher the course, the more William enjoys it.

Polo is a sport the prince also enjoys. During the summer of 2000, William did practise stick-and-balling on his father's ponies under the watchful eye of an Argentinian instructor, took part in practice chukkas and had a few matches. Since returning from Africa in 2001, William has devoted many hours to polo and has improved greatly under expert tuition.

Once again, William is attracted to the sport simply because he sees it as a challenge. It is accepted that polo is one of the world's most difficult sports, and playing top-class polo is demanding and highly dangerous, requiring not only skill and riding ability but also a good eye and, most importantly, great courage. He has learned the hard way that the polo field is not for softies.

William discovered that fact during the summer of 2001, during which he had a couple of spills and several near misses. But he never seriously injured himself and on each occasion he was thrown, William collected himself, checked his helmet, dusted himself down and got straight back in the saddle.

He readily confesses, 'It's not the pony's fault I end up on the ground, but my fault. Sometimes I try to turn too tightly or reach too far for a ball. The point is that I'm not yet that good, but I will be one day.'

He has said, 'I know that when you make a basic mistake at polo a player often ends up being punished, either by falling off or completely missing the ball and feeling a complete idiot.'

William occasionally enjoys a day's fly fishing in the River Dee at Balmoral where he is accompanied by a first-class gillie, the men who know every nook and cranny of that part of the river. William is happy enough to be on his own standing thigh-high in the icy waters in his green waders for hours at a time with a gillie for advice and company.

For years, William and Harry accompanied their parents on skiing trips to Klosters in Switzerland for two weeks around the New Year, but not in 2001. After Charles and Diana separated, the two lads went skiing with Charles most years and, on occasions, with Tiggy Legge-Bourke and a couple of friends. Both William and Harry enjoyed those holidays but only when the paparazzi kept their distance.

In December 2000, when William returned from Patagonia, Charles asked the lads if they wanted to go skiing and, somewhat to his surprise, they both decided to stay in England. Charles, who has always been a keen skier, was rather taken aback by their decision. He felt somewhat miffed and so he, too, decided not to take a January skiing holiday. It seemed that William's keenness to shoot and ride had taken precedence over a more glamorous, but more public, sport of skiing.

Throughout his gap year, William wanted, above all else, to stay out of the limelight and enjoy a quiet life. He didn't want to offer the photographers any opportunity to take pictures of him unless he had agreed to the photo shoot weeks beforehand. Even then, William usually agreed to such photo shoots only after his father had talked to him about the need for such pictures.

When he wasn't hunting, riding or

fishing, William would often lie in bed in the morning, get up late, read a newspaper or turn on the TV. He would saunter down to a late breakfast and then hang around, go for a walk with the dogs, or get on the phone to mates. He also enjoyed screaming around Highgrove on his motorbike which he hopes he will be allowed to take to St Andrews in September.

One reason William wants to take his motorbike to St Andrews is to thwart paparazzi photographers, because he would be able to ride around the town incognito, hidden from view wearing his crash helmet. Such a method of making life as difficult as possible for the paparazzi really appeals to William who still harbours feelings of bitterness and enmity towards them.

Undoubtedly, William has matured appreciably during the last 12 months and his interests have changed dramatically. Many of his earlier sporting interests seem to have been forgotten or put to one side. He now shows little or no interest in swimming or rowing in which he had shown such great promise in his days at Eton. Nowadays,

William will occasionally go for a swim but it seems he has no interest in trying to perfect his skills, swim competitively or develop the techniques for which he won considerable praise and many prizes swimming for Eton.

And the same goes for rowing. William is a natural oarsman and achieved a high standard rowing successfully for Eton during his final year. Indeed, both rowing and swimming were responsible for enabling William to develop such strong shoulders, back, arms and legs at such a young age. But throughout his gap year, William hardly went near a boat and appeared to have no inclination to take to the water. He had other things on his mind — adventure, travel and excitement.

3

The Party-goer

At the start of his gap year, William had promised himself to achieve one ambition. He confided to a few mates that he was determined to find a really good-looking, fun-loving girlfriend so that they could hang around together enjoying life. And he did meet many teenage girls and young 20-somethings at the occasional parties he attended and at the homes of Eton pals he visited.

He is no different from any other young teenage lad. Whenever attending such parties,

William would take great care to look 'the part', spending time selecting the right clothes for the occasion. He much preferred attending informal parties where he could dress casually, following the current teenage fashion, favouring light cotton trousers with no crease, a T-shirt under an open-necked shirt worn outside the trousers, and casual shoes.

Somewhat to his disappointment, however, William found he was usually invited to rather formal parties where parents hung about in another part of the mansion — or large London house — and the young men were expected to be smart rather than casual, and wear ties and sometimes dinner suits. Invariably, he found the girls dressed in party outfits.

At all these parties, of course, William was the centre of attention and he didn't like that. He wanted to be accepted as just 'one of the boys', not a royal prince. But that proved impossible and it annoyed him.

'But he does love girls flocking around him,' commented James, 19, one of his close

Eton pals. 'I've watched him at a party standing in a kitchen with a beer in his hand chatting to a group of five or six girls. He's laughing, cracking jokes, flashing that 'come-on' smile and the girls are drooling over him. On those occasions, the shy William is nowhere to be seen. He's loving the attention. He certainly joins in the chit-chat, laughing, cracking jokes and giving the girls his sexy look.

'He also loves to shock them. His trick is to say something totally outrageous which those standing around would never believe William would never dream of saying.

'Wills will shock them by using really bad language and he invariably uses swear words in his everyday conversation with mates. To his mates, especially those he knew well at Eton, he's just one of the boys and there is nothing he likes more than that.

'As a result, he talks the way we all talk. Of course we use bad language; that's taken for granted. The same goes for William as well. The fact that he is heir to the throne doesn't make a blind bit of difference to him. He's just one of us.

'William is also renowned for holding girls' attention by cracking really rude, sexy jokes. At first, the girls are totally taken aback. You can see that by the look on their faces. They don't seem to know whether they should laugh or not, because most believe that butter wouldn't melt in his mouth. But they quickly came to really enjoy his rather crude, sex-orientated jokes because he was showing he was one of them, not some stuck-up young royal.'

In that way, of course, William takes after his mother. Amongst her inner circle, Princess Diana became well known for her sense of humour, which generally revolved around either sex or food and sometimes both! Diana liked being really crude because she knew it surprised, sometimes astonished, those to whom she was telling the joke. Most people who met Diana believed her to be too pure, innocent and uncorruptable to indulge in such crudity. Far from it. She enjoyed shocking people and used crude jokes about sexual matters to do so.

And she would do so not just to friends and acquaintances, but to junior members of her staff, aircraft cabin crews or charity officials who would generally blush bright red, not knowing where to look or whether to laugh or turn away in embarrassment. After making such a joke, Diana would roar with laughter and, of course, her audience would take their cue from her and laugh, too.

And, like his mother, William also enjoys hearing dirty jokes with all the four-letter words thrown in for good measure. Like Diana, William will then roar with laughter in great guffaws rather than quiet chuckles. And so it was with Diana. But it was a Diana whom only a few people knew because most hadn't the nerve to crack rude jokes to the Princess of Wales unless they knew her very well.

Most of William's pals and acquaintances and those who work around him, now understand that the 19-year-old prince has certainly matured in the past 12 months and have discovered that he gets a kick out of lavatory humour as well as sexually explicit jokes.

At all the parties William attended during his gap year food and drink and plenty of smoking were a matter of course. William discovered that it was mostly the young lads who drank too much and the girls who did most of the cigarette smoking. Like his mother, William used to believe smoking was antisocial and bad for people's health. He would try and persuade friends to stop smoking but no more. Now William enjoys the occasional cigarette which he finds relaxing. And he has ceased his anti-smoking crusade.

Drugs are definitely a no-no for William, as they were for his mother and father, but he doesn't comment about drug-taking among any of his mates. He knows that some do and some don't, but he simply believes that it's none of his business and he doesn't want to know. In that way, there can be no embarrassment for him or his friends. He knows some people do drugs at parties, but he has let it be known that he doesn't want anything to do with the drugs scene.

While having a beer or two with his mates at such parties, William spent quite a lot of time discussing and commenting on the girls. James, who attended a number of such parties, said, 'Most of the time, Wills is simply too choosey. He always finds fault with a girl he fancies and then goes off her without attempting to get to know her properly.

' He likes the girls to make the running, to take the initiative, to give him the eye before he zeroes in. And, of course, because he is Prince William, very few girls have the balls to do that. As a result, Wills will sometimes go to a party and simply chat with pals in the kitchen, but at other times he does really enter into the spirit. I have seen him go wild on a few occasions, but I've never actually seen him totally pissed, out of his head. Like all of us, he sometimes has one too many but that just makes him laugh more. I've never seen him drunk but I have seen him tipsy.'

When William invited people around for a small drinks party, he wanted nothing elaborate. He wanted drinks and a few things people could eat from a side-table, like nuts, crisps or slices of pizza. He didn't want waiters or footmen hanging around because he believed that would ruin the informality of the party and his young guests would then behave differently, as though on parade rather than enjoying themselves and letting their hair down as they did at most of the other get-togethers.

James commented, 'What Wills loves are pretty wild parties in private where everyone does everything with no inhibitions. And that includes getting drunk, snogging in public or going off into a room with a girl for whatever. But, unfortunately for Wills, we are hardly ever invited to those sorts of parties.

'Wills always hoped that, at the parties he attends, the parents would have taken the hint and gone off for the evening. But that hardly ever happens. Wills knows that having parents hanging around, even in a different part of the house, puts a real damper on the evening. The trouble for poor Wills is that some parents want an opportunity to see Wills at close quarters and chat to him, perhaps get to know him. That's the last thing Wills wants!'

4

Wills Roughs It

Months before leaving Eton, William had decided to take a gap year and spend some time on his own, away from friends and family, away from England, away from the pressures of being a perfectly behaved teenager, the heir to the throne.

William has never enjoyed the spotlight and never sought it. Today, he still doesn't. Whenever he has to be 'on parade', turning out as a member of 'the Firm', posing for pictures, he thoroughly dislikes the prospect.

When younger, William used to become almost sick with nerves whenever he had to appear in public in front of the cameras.

As a toddler and as a child, William enjoyed running around for the cameras, intrigued by everything going on around him. By the age of ten, however, he had taken a distinct dislike to cameras and photographers because he was then old enough to see the affect photographers had on his mother.

As William explained to an Eton friend, 'When you've seen your mother come home in tears because she was being pursued by bloody photographers, you can understand why I hated them so much. I used to feel sick in the pit of my stomach whenever I had to perform in front the cameras. I hated that. It was the worst part of growing up.'

He explained how that intense distrust had led to his awkward teenage phase when he simply refused to co-operate in front of the cameras even when his parents pleaded with him to do so. It wasn't that he was being deliberately awkward, but that he wanted both his parents to understand that he hated posing for photographs because he so hated photographers. He didn't believe that the press and TV companies should have the right to poke their cameras into his private life the way they had done to his mother, making her life a 'living hell' throughout her adult life.

He added, 'I still don't like posing for the cameras, but when I have to do so, I do it. Really, I do it just to please my father. I look on it as a duty. That doesn't mean I enjoy it but I understand that it is a necessity, a duty. Tough.'

For months, William and his Eton pals had discussed how they would spend their gap year. Everyone, of course, had different ideas. William just wanted to get as far away as possible from his life as a royal pursued by cameramen. He talked to his father, Camilla and Harry as well as friends outside Eton — Tom Parker Bowles, Camilla's son; Peter Phillips, Princess Anne's son; 21-year-old William van Cutsem; and his two other cousins Zara Phillips, 20, and Gabriella Windsor, 20, daughter of Prince and Princess Michael of Kent.

William was given so much advice he wasn't at all sure what he should do, except that he knew he wanted to escape. He wanted to get away from everyone and everything. He certainly didn't want to go anywhere in the world where he would be recognised; he simply wanted to disappear 'off the face of the earth' so that he could be himself.

It was Prince Charles who came up with the idea of William going to some distant foreign land with Raleigh International, for he had been responsible, with the adventurer Colonel John Blashford Snell, for setting up the original 'Operation Raleigh' in 1984. Though Charles is not the patron of Raleigh International, he has always kept a watchful eye on its remarkable progress.

In their brochure, Raleigh state, 'We inspire people from all backgrounds and nationalities to discover their full potential by working together on challenging environmental and community projects around the world.'

It continues, 'A Raleigh International expedition is a unique journey of exploration;

of beautiful and remote places, of different peoples and cultures. Perhaps, most importantly, it is also an exploration of yourself and a development of your true potential.'

The ten-week-long experience could have been tailor-made for William, for it promised living and sharing in the lives of other communities and working with people of all backgrounds and nationalities. William could have chosen Costa Rica, Mongolia, Belize, Namibia or Ghana but he fancied the idea of working in Chile, a part of the world he had never visited. His ten-week sojourn in southern Chile at a peasant village named Tortel in the foothills of the Patagonian mountains would prove a far cry from the privileged life he had spent in royal palaces and wealthy stately homes and the cloistered confines of Eton College.

And the people were totally different. No sovereigns or princes, no royal servants or stuffed shirts, no politicians and no members of the wealthy privileged classes.

When William returned home before

Christmas 2000, he chatted enthusiastically to a number of friends about his ten weeks of 'great fun but jolly hard work' in Patagonia.

And what he *really* enjoyed was being away from everyone he had ever known in his life, including his family. He explained to a former Etonian, 'At boarding school you are away from your parents and your normal home life routine but you're still surrounded by people you know. The boys you get to know in that first term remain with you as you all move up through the school together. By and large, they were great guys but, understandably, most treated me with kid gloves, not sure how they should behave.

'But in England, I'm always treated with kid gloves as though I'm someone special and I hate that. I wish people treated me as just an ordinary teenager growing up fast. But they don't; they never do. And, to be honest, it's bloody awful.

'In Patagonia, the local people didn't know me from Adam. They treated me the same as they treated the other 100 young people in the group. It was wonderful to be treated like that, as one of the Raleigh lads helping out. I didn't want to be treated differently; I didn't want any special privileges and I never got any. Great!

'I asked everyone connected with the expedition to simply call me William, or Wills, including all the villagers and their children. And everyone did. That was important because I just felt like one of a team, no one special. To me it was the most amazing ten weeks of my life because I could be 'me' and just mess around like everyone else. It was a revelation to me. I would go back next year if I could.'

In fact, the only part of the trip William didn't look forward to was the week the media arrived. He had agreed that, for a few days, a camera crew could come to Tortel to film him at work. In fact, a camera crew was the last thing William wanted to see but he knew he had to go through with the ordeal though he didn't exactly enjoy it. And he had promised his father there would be no tantrums. There were none.

'For one thing, I had to wear a hard hat,'

he said with a laugh. 'It was the only time I ever wore one. Stupid really. We're meant to live like the locals and work like the locals. Then they made me wear a hard hat for the filming, something the locals have never worn in their entire lives. It just made a mockery of the whole exercise.'

Indeed, William did live in exactly the same way and in the same conditions, carrying out the same work, doing the same mundane domestic duties, eating the same food and mucking in along with the other 100 young people and the 40-odd volunteer staff on the ten-week-long expedition. Indeed, he happily took his turn cleaning out the lavatories and washing the floors, something he had never in his life had ever been called upon to do!

One of the expedition's main projects was to build a series of sturdy wooden walkways above the marshland linking the villagers' homes and to construct an extension to the village fire station.

From all reports, William entered into the cut and thrust of the work with great enthusiasm, seeking no privileges and asking that no quarter be given. He volunteered for the toughest jobs, like carrying the heaviest logs and slogging away at digging the trenches and holes required. He didn't shirk from carrying out the most menial of tasks and, whenever heavy work had to be carried out, William would always volunteer. And, when necessary, he was always prepared to work that extra hour longer to make sure a job was completed on time.

William not only joined in with everyone else, sharing all the various duties, but the great majority of those taking part readily accepted his natural leadership abilities which he had, of course, learned and honed as a prefect during his final year at Eton. During those 12 months, William had revealed natural leadership skills which surfaced again during those ten weeks of voluntary work in Patagonia. As a result, William won respect not only from the technical staff but also from everyone taking part in the expedition no matter what their nationality, their background or their skills.

The expedition consisted of three separate phases — community, adventure and environment.

He said later, 'From my point of view, the community phase was the most interesting and creative. It was certainly my favourite. I felt that, for once in my life, I was helping to make a difference, a real difference, to people's lives. You build things which they need, desperately need. The Raleigh staff have the necessary skills and we volunteers provide the labour. Some of the time, the work is really hard graft but, because you realise you are helping to improve people's lives, you take a great pride in it. It's hard but intensely enjoyable. And you can see how much Raleigh's work is appreciated.

'The people even invited us into their homes and made us feel really welcome and yet we couldn't communicate by language because we didn't understand their tongue and they certainly didn't understand English. But it didn't seem to matter because you do understand their kindness and generosity and their appreciation for the work we were carrying out for them.

'Everyone got along so well despite the language barrier probably because the villagers were so friendly. You didn't need words and yet we communicated really well.'

But William's ten weeks 'away-from-it-all' expedition began on a disastrous note.

Along with 11 other adventurers William was thrown into the deep end, instructed to take part in the adventure phase of the expedition, a seven-day exploration in kayaks along the rugged and desolate southern Patagonia coastline. The group had been scheduled to spend three weeks away from the main camp situated in the village of Tortel, exploring the deep ocean fjords and archipelagos that dot the dramatic, rugged coastline.

The plan was to spend three weeks living in a total wilderness, miles from any civilization, near a village named Punto Mano, while they detailed the activities of such wildlife as dolphins, sea lions and the fabled condors. William had never before lived in such conditions and he was eagerly looking forward to the adventure.

But during the months of October and November, the southern part of Patagonia is notorious for wild, rough weather conditions with force six to eight storms, lashing rain and high seas. And William and his team found themselves facing those horrendous weather conditions in the first 24 hours. William and his fellow venturers would be sorely tested, having to live together in atrocious conditions for five days. It became a test of their morale, their stamina and their character. They hadn't expected anything like it.

William later revealed what had happened. 'On the first day, we paddled in our kayaks against a rising storm for three hours simply to reach the first scheduled land base, a safe beach where we could pull up our kayaks away from the seas.

'We had hardly finished that task when the rain began to come down in torrents.'

With some difficulty, the group managed to pitch their tents — a difficult job in storm-force wind — and have their first meal. Outside, the rain lashed down and the wind was ripping at the tents. That night, they crawled into their sleeping bags exhausted and lay there listening to the howling wind and the torrential rain.

The following morning, there had been no change in the weather. William said later, 'Unbelievably, the rain never stopped, never stopped for five days and five nights. You go to bed, you wake up, it's still raining. We were all soaked through.

'We thought of trying to leave the beach and paddle our kayaks further down the coast but there was no way we could launch the kayaks into such big waves. The sea was simply too rough. There was another point. We hadn't, of course, had much practice paddling kayaks and we weren't that good. So we had to stay put.

'We had to go to bed each night in wet clothes but, thank goodness, my sleeping bag somehow remained dry, which was a great relief. Eventually, even the tent became wet through; it was saturated.

'In the end, we became quite demoralised even though we somehow managed to keep ourselves going by singing, telling jokes and stories, playing games like I-Spy and things like that.

'Of course, we also had to eat and try to keep warm. Some of the venturers so hated the rain they stayed in their tents all day and all night, hardly ever going out. That meant that only a few of us had to take it in turns to go out into the blinding rain, chopping and collecting fire wood. Lighting fires was particularly difficult but, once we got it going, the fire cheered everyone up.

'The thing was, I'd never seen rain like that before in my life. It was so heavy and it just didn't stop. To make matters worse, there was a howling wind as well — the tents were flapping around and almost blowing away. It was touch and go. Thank goodness our two tents didn't become flooded because that would have been disastrous.

'It became quite demoralising. I think we all felt wretched. Everyone was thinking to themselves, "Why? Why did I choose to come here?" But we somehow managed to get through it. And that was good.'

After five sodden days the 12 venturers — six young men and women — awoke to find the rain had finally ceased. When they looked out of their bivouacs, they saw blue sky.

The first job was to light a fire, dry out their clothes and, at the same time, get themselves warmed through for the first time since pitching their tents. As their clothes dried and their cold, wet bodies warmed up, their spirits, too, began to rise and they enjoyed their best meal for a long time. So good did they feel that, later that day, they launched their kayaks and enjoyed the exercise in the heat of the sun.

William didn't exactly enjoy the adventure phase of the expedition. As he put it later in his own words, 'It was bloody awful, ghastly.'

The next phase of William's Chilean adventure was far more fun and far more interesting, tracking an endangered species of deer across the Patagonian plains. For three weeks, William, accompanied by ten other young people, roamed the Tamango National Reserve tracking the rare huemul deer whose numbers have been dwindling over the past decade. Using a combination of radio beacons and more traditional tracking methods the venturers walked miles each day. At night, they cooked round a camp fire and slept in three-man tents or under the stars.

The third part of his expedition was not so tough. He settled into single-storey accomodation in the remote and unspoilt village of Tortel, so isolated that it can only be reached by boat or aircraft. But it wasn't exactly palatial. He slept with 15 other young men all crammed like tinned sardines on the cold, concrete floor of a drab old nursery classroom. He shared his padded mat with four others next to a grubby, off-white wall covered in children's crayon drawings.

William would later recall that he enjoyed this part of the expedition more than the others because he felt he was really helping the indigenous population — who lead hard, exacting, short lives — to enjoy a better life. With the other volunteers, he helped to build wooden walkways above the swampy ground so that all parts of the village were accessible to everyone all the year round. In Tortel, of course, there were no cars and roads. He also helped to build an extension to the village's small fire station.

Those four weeks in Tortel also brought William into daily contact with the locals and he spent hours delighting the children, chatting to them in his imperfect Spanish which made many of them laugh at his attempts. He didn't mind at all. He played games with the youngsters and happily threw himself into all of their dance routines.

That also made them laugh, particularly the young girls who seemed to know exactly how to dance the salsa.

Marie Wright, 29, the Raleigh project manager in Tortel, commented, 'William earned the respect of the venturers and staff and was very well liked. He was popular on his own merits. He got on with the work and what impressed us all was that he showed he was humble. He appeared rather laid back and never once did he make any reference to his family or his background.'

Expedition leader, Malcolm Sutherland commented, 'William was very popular. He's got a very personable approach to life and he was happy to get stuck into everything the group was doing.'

William said, 'I did the Raleigh expedition not because I wanted to find myself or anything like that, but because it was different. I didn't do it because I wanted to change myself. I never thought I was going to like Raleigh but it grew on me, especially doing the community work. That's the part I really enjoyed.'

William continued, 'I suppose I chose Raleigh to be involved in an expedition because I wanted to do something totally different from anything I had ever done in my life. I didn't want to sit around and get a job or something back in London. I wanted to get out and see a bit of the world as well as doing something to help other people who hadn't got very much. It was also a really good way of meeting lots of other people from other backgrounds.'

He certainly did that. The group was as

diverse as could be imagined. There was a 17-year-old lad who was trying to escape from a life of drugs; a 19-year-old woman who was considered 'at risk'; an 18-year-old lad who was trying to end a life of petty crime; middle-class kids from good homes and stable backgrounds; a 23-year-old Cambridge graduate; a 33-year-old female doctor; a 24-year-old Customs officer from Arabia; and a 26-year-old female accountant from Hong Kong. There were also many young people taking a gap year like William.

With everyone else, William lived, ate and slept in the leaky-roofed nursery where the only furniture was a bare wooden table with four benches, a play frame and a couple of slides for young children. These were draped with the volunteers' clothes, as it was the only place to put them.

The 16 shared two lavatories, but only one was working. The other would not flush and had no seat. The only shower consisted of a five-gallon water bag dangling from a bamboo frame wrapped with a blue tarpaulin.

The dining area at the other end of the

single-storey hut was lined with cardboard boxes which contained their food supplies — potatoes, carrots, onions and tins of powdered milk. The volunteers ate from lightweight mess tins with spoons and these hung on hooks on a wooden board nailed to the wall.

William also took his turn cooking and everyone washed up. The kitchen contained a large iron wood-burning stove and an ankle-high wobbly bench on which condiments were kept. Washing-up was carried out on the porch in a pair of well-worn plastic tubs filled with cold water.

William commented, 'We nicknamed this place Hotel Tortel. After our week of hell trapped on the beach in the torrential rain, our old nursery seemed like a luxury hotel.'

The only type-written notice declared that alcohol was banned, as well as any relationships between staff and Raleigh volunteers. It warned that any such relationships would lead to both being sent home.

William confessed later, 'I did find living with 15 total strangers rather difficult to start with. I had never had such an experience before in my life. It was impossible to have any privacy or any secrets from anyone. At first, I found it all rather embarrassing. I'm a very private person and I found it rather awkward, but I got used to it. We shared everything, absolutely everything. In the end, I learned to deal with it.'

William also won praise for tackling a fire which destroyed a camp shelter and threatened to burn all the group's kit which was stored there. The fire started accidentally when a freak gust of wind ignited the wooden shelter which only had a tarpaulin roof. William ran to the burning shelter and, with no thought for his own safety, ran inside to rescue all the group's gear. Three times he went back into the flames and managed to rescue everything. In fact, William was fortunate to escape without any burns because the thermal top he was wearing at the time was burned by the flames as he ran from the building.

In a bid to save the shelter, William and another young man grabbed two plastic containers and ran to the nearby river where they filled the buckets and ran back to the blazing building. William then realised there was a real danger that an adjoining building would also be burned to the ground as the flames swept towards it.

So William grabbed an axe and began smashing the burning building to the ground so the flames could not spread while the other young man, a Raleigh medic, kept refilling the plastic containers and throwing the water on to the flames.

For 15 minutes, William and the medic fought the blaze on their own, saving all the equipment as well as the adjoining building. The two young men were still trying to put out the flames when the rest of the group returned. When they saw what was happening, they, too, joined in fighting the fire, running back and forth from the river to the shelter with buckets of water. Ten minutes later, the blaze was out.

Those on the trip praised William for the risks he took in saving their equipment and the way he and the medic fought the fire, but

William wanted no praise. 'I just did what anyone else would have done in the circumstances,' he said. 'I was just glad I was there at the time.'

Looking back on his ten-week expedition to Patagonia, William is pleased that he went and enjoyed the experience, but he hasn't decided whether he would want to become involved in any further trips. He told friends, 'I am really glad that I did it. The place was fantastic, a totally different world and that was great. But now I've done it I'm not sure I would want to repeat the adventure. It was a once-in-a-lifetime experience and I'm really pleased I went through with it. I think it was good for me.

'I chose Chile because I had never been to South America and I wanted to go somewhere colder rather than hotter. I also wanted to go somewhere different, somewhere I would probably never visit in my lifetime. I was really fortunate in choosing Chile. It is a beautiful, wild country, so very different from London. I liked that. Chile boasts magnificent scenery and I found the Chilean people charming and remarkably happy. They seemed so natural, with no airs or graces. I loved that about them. And they were so friendly and fun-loving and appreciative of what we were doing for them. They really are lovely people and the children are beautiful.'

5

Big Game Hunter

Without a doubt, the highlight of William's gap year was the two months he spent on safari in southern Africa, and the best part of that was the thrill and excitement of big game hunting, tracking and shooting a variety of wild animals.

During these safaris in the wildlife paradise of Botswana, Wills personally took part in culling a wide range of animals, including wildebeest, warthogs, bushpig and a variety of antelope, including springbok and reedbuck.

He spent days living rough while tracking more exotic species like the common waterbuck, nyala, the Hartmann zebra and eland which can roam for scores of miles across the vast Botswana plains, in areas the size of Ireland.

William spoke to Charles and Harry during long telephone calls back home telling of his 'fantastic' holiday living rough under canvas and taking an active part in stalking and culling the wild animals. On his return, William has been full of stories of those adventures. Big game hunting has become William's most treasured interest.

William told pals, 'Those safaris have been the most incredible time of my entire life. Absolutely wicked.'

For the first part of his African adventure, William was accompanied by Mark Dyer, the former Welsh Guards officer.

During the first part of their African trip, William and Mark took part in wildlife conservation safaris in which they tracked and shot wild animals, but only with tranquilising darts so that vets could then check and examine them and take blood samples.

In the Okavango Delta region of Botswana, however, William has been accompanied by professional game hunters and trackers. He was granted a licence from the Botswana Government to take part in safaris, shooting wild game.

William spent most nights under canvas hundreds of miles from civilization. On occasions, they stayed in lodge-type camps, which are permanent buildings with all mod cons.

They travelled in 4x4 vehicles across the open plains but spent some time on foot stalking the game, sometimes tramping miles over rough terrain. Sometimes they rode on horseback. It was exhausting but thrilling.

Most nights, of course, the team would return to their canvas tents and enjoy an excellent dinner cooked by a chef who also joined the small, exclusive royal party. The chef, who is frequently employed for safari shooting parties, would on occasion cook the game that had been hunted and killed by

Prince William.

According to reports, William sometimes came across wild pigs and wild boar which unexpectedly shot out from the undergrowth. William and the professional hunters needed to be fast and accurate with their shots.

He was well aware that such wild boar and pigs can be extremely dangerous when they feel threatened because they are very fast over short distances and ferocious when aroused. They have been known to kill grown men. On his return, William told friends of some of his more hair-raising experiences in the bush when the party came across wild boar.

Botswana safaris are respected by big game hunters as among the very best in the world and many government safari guides take parties of hunters around the country culling the vast herds of wild game that roam the plains. Government licences are issued and the culling is strictly under the auspices of the qualified trackers and hunters. The expensive Government licences, which are rationed, give the hunter permission to cull certain wildlife depending on numbers, the time of year, the condition of the herds and the rainfall.

The months of April and May usually provide the best hunting in Botswana when the rainy season ends and when the vegetation is thick and water abundant. This causes the game to be widespread and at times difficult to spot, making the hunting of some species particularly challenging.

In Botswana, William discovered the height of his ambition. He found hunting big game gave him a tremendous surge of adrenalin and was far more exciting and intoxicating than he had ever thought possible.

William not only enjoyed the challenge of stalking and shooting the wild animals, but the fact that he was also pitting his hunting skills against quarries which knew every inch of cover. And the longer and more difficult the pursuit of his quarry, the more William relished the challenge.

By big game hunting in Botswana, William was following in his father's footsteps. Before he was married, Prince Charles visited southern Africa on a couple of occasions on hunting safaris and had really enjoyed the thrill of tracking and killing a variety of wild animals, including wildebeest, antelope, warthog and bushpig.

Charles understood William's desire to test his skill as a hunter and a marksmen in the toughest, most difficult terrain where game can be killed with impunity. So William took his father's advice and thoroughly enjoyed the trip of his lifetime.

6

Unhappy at Home

During 2001, William has become unhappy, miserable and downhearted living at Highgrove. He has complained to friends that he sometimes feels like a stranger in his own home, the one place where he had come to find happiness and security.

Shortly after the trauma of his mother's death, William discovered to his joy that he and Harry had become much closer to their father. William talked of a strong relationship, a new affinity between the three of them.

In the months that followed, a new, closer and deeper relationship developed with his father which William had never before experienced. That new relationship helped William come to terms with the tragedy of his mother's death.

William found he really enjoyed the time he spent with his father. He looked forward to seeing him, to their chats, their meals together and their outings together, whether it was shooting, fishing or simply taking the dogs for a walk. He felt at home. He felt close to him.

Indeed, his new-found relationship with Charles gave William a greater confidence than ever before. He felt positive, more self-assured and less fearful of his future life.

As a friend of the family put it, 'No longer did William and Harry have to divide their lives and their feelings between their competing parents, for now they only had one home and one parent and they both came to treasure that fact. William felt it was a new beginning which he never wanted to lose.'

Understandably, both lads had been shocked and emotionally devastated by Diana's death and Charles had become a real strength in their young lives, happy to be at their beck and call because he understood what his sons were going through. He knew that the sudden death of Diana could have a terrible and lasting effect on them and he wanted to do all in his power to alleviate their feelings of loss and despair.

Charles knew from bitter personal experience what it was like to grow up with parents who were virtual strangers. He had grown up never having felt the love of a close-knit family. And he had yearned for love from both his parents. He was only four years of age when his grandfather, King George VI, died and his mother became Queen.

As a result, she could never again spend the time she might have wanted with Charles and her other children. As a result, of course, Charles never felt close to his mother, though he admired her greatly and respected her. He still does.

Unfortunately, Charles had a disastrous relationship with his father. Prince Philip offered Charles little paternal affection. He treated Charles more like a midshipman in the Royal Navy than his own beloved son. Indeed, Charles had always felt that his father had sent him to the toughest of boarding schools, Gordonstoun in Scotland, more as a punishment than an education. Charles didn't enjoy his years at Gordonstoun, neither did he enjoy his holidays back home at Buckingham Palace.

With the death of Diana, Charles had the opportunity to be the father he always wanted to be. He determined that William and Harry should enjoy their lives and understand that their father loved them above all else.

For his part, Charles wanted the boys to enjoy the benefits of a real home where they could be themselves, enjoy themselves, play around, watch TV, listen to their favourite music, invite their friends round and relax. He never forgot his own stiff, formal, unhappy childhood during which he had to behave correctly at all times.

Charles wanted his boys to look on Highgrove as their home, the family home, in contrast to earlier times when Highgrove was simply their father's home, where they felt like weekend visitors.

Both William and Harry spent most of their young lives floating between a number of homes, not only dividing their lives between Highgrove and Kensington Palace but also staying for a few weeks at a time at Windsor Castle, Sandringham or Balmoral. And from the age of seven, they were both away at boarding schools.

William could recall the old days, coming home from boarding school not knowing what to expect; not certain whether he would be staying at Highgrove or Kensington Palace, not knowing how long he would be with his father or his mother. He had hated that feeling of divided loyalty. He had always felt guilty that he might be favouring one parent more than the other.

Charles determined to fill the gap in their emotional lives, to make them feel wanted and secure in a happy home environment. Charles showed he cared for them and loved them. Their place was to be with him at Highgrove.

As a result, a deep friendship developed between Charles and his sons which hadn't existed before. It seemed to William that the tragedy of the death of his mother had brought them closer together and that gave him a warm feeling, and greater confidence.

William, of course, had hated the arguments, the anger and the emotional turmoil that had ravaged his young life as his parents argued and fought. He hated even more the fact that their separation and divorce had been played out in public for the world to see. He hated the newspaper headlines. On occasions, William was physically sick when reading stories of his parents break-up.

But now, William only had one home, Highgrove, and he loved it. Now there were no more painful arguments, no more feelings that he was in the middle of a tug-of-war which had always made him sad and which he had always hated. William recalled the times he had gone to bed in tears solely because his parents had spent their time together rowing and arguing, occasions when Diana had ended up screaming and crying and Charles was permanentlyin a rage he tried to hide. All that was behind him, gone for ever.

William loved the fact that he now had a home like all his Eton friends. He felt a warmth in his heart that he could talk about 'home' the way other boys did. Through the horrible death of his beloved mother, William had found the comfort, peace and security for which he had always yearned. Now he felt he belonged somewhere that was special to him and to Harry, a real home they could call their own.

At *exeat* weekends, half-term and the end of the school term, William looked forward with happiness and excitement to going home. He was looking forward to seeing Harry, chatting to his father, just being with them both, as well as the more exciting activities on the agenda like hunting, shooting, fishing, riding his motorbike and going walks with the dogs. All these activities William now enjoyed with Charles and Harry as a small, tight-knit family and he felt secure.

Indeed, in the bad old days, William often hoped that he would not stay with either his mother or his father, but preferred instead to spend the holidays or weekends with Tiggy Legge-Bourke, the young woman brought in to act as a soul-mate after Diana and Charles had separated for good. From the start, William had found Tiggy a great sport, someone who was absolutely open and easy to talk to and confide in. With Tiggy, there never appeared to be any problems.

Over time, William built up a good, open relationship with Tiggy for she was someone whom he trusted. They had fun together; they laughed together and Tiggy made his life enjoyable. William would recall with happiness their times together tramping through the fields or the woods, searching for rabbits to shoot or, in Scotland, stalking the deer, riding out or going on picnics together in the summer months.

So Tiggy became even more important in William's life. She became the person to whom William turned to in moments of doubt and crisis. He asked her all the questions for which he needed answers, such as the fights and problems between his parents. And Tiggy explained as best she could what was going on trying to reassure the young boy. Tiggy was always there to offer sympathy and comfort, friendship and understanding. When things got too much for William, she also became a shoulder for him to cry on. And on many occasions, he did so.

The feeling of security that William had treasured with Tiggy he now discovered with Charles. As a consequence, a strong bond has developed between them both, something deeper and stronger than William had known before. He felt good about it with no sense of guilt that had been so much a part of his early childhood. He was happy at last, very happy.

But that was before Camilla moved into Highgrove.

Of course, both William and Harry knew of their father's relationship with Camilla. They had known her nearly all their lives. To both boys, Camilla had seemed like a sort of aunt, a well-meaning, quiet, sensible, horsey-type of woman whom they saw from time to time.

From a young age, William and Harry had visited her home, Middlewick House, a seven-bedroom country mansion near Highgrove where she lived with her husband, Andrew, and their children Tom (who is five years older than William) and Laura (who is two years older). William, in particular, got on really well with Tom and enjoyed playing with him. Tom became a sort of surrogate elder brother and William liked that. All four members of the Parker Bowles family had been frequent guests at Highgrove.

Indeed, in those far-off days, Camilla and Diana were friendly to one another, two mothers with young children to discuss, chat about and compare. Diana frequently turned to Camilla, who was some 13 years older, for advice about the children and they chatted like any other mums about their children and their differences, their problems and illnesses, their likes and dislikes. Camilla knew all about William and Harry.

With the breakdown of her marriage, Diana came to know about Charles's life-long relationship with Camilla. Only at that stage did Diana finally come to understand that Charles and Camilla had been lovers some years before. She realised at last for how long — some 20 years — the two had been alternately lovers, friends and, at times merely acquaintances. Understandably, she was upset and angry that Charles had never told her the whole truth.

But in the months following Diana's death, Camilla hardly ever visited Highgrove during school holidays when William and Harry were at home or during *exeat* weekends. In no way did she want the young princes to see her as an interloper in the close-knit family unit of Charles and his two teenage lads.

Sensibly, Camilla kept well away whenever the boys were at Highgrove, only occasionally dropping in to see them for a cup of coffee, afternoon tea or the occasional meal. But nothing more.

In front of the boys, there were little or no signs of affection between Charles and Camilla. She would chat to the boys about school, their studies and their school sports, as well as the riding, fishing and shooting they enjoyed at home. All safe territory, but nevertheless an important contact point in building a good relationship between Camilla and the boys. Sometimes, Camilla came over to Highgrove with Tom and Laura and, as before, they got on famously with William and Harry.

But when the boys were away at their respective boarding schools, Camilla became a more frequent visitor. At first, Camilla hardly ever stayed over but then, as the weeks became months, her visits became more frequent, and the infrequent stays became more lengthy. But not when the lads were due home.

Finally, during the summer of 1999, nearly two years after Diana's death, Camilla moved into Highgrove lock, stock and barrel. In retrospect, it now seems that decision may have been premature for neither William nor Harry welcomed the fact Camilla was now living at Highgrove.

Importantly, neither boy felt they had gained a 'new' mother but feared they had lost their father who had so recently become a source of strength to both of them.

At a stroke, William felt that Camilla's permanent presence at Highgrove had ruined the relationship which he had so enjoyed when Charles was living there alone. All the little things, like the three of them having meals together, going for walks with the dogs, chatting, playing cards, watching television, doing just about everything together, all of that had gone. Gone for ever. And William hated it.

As a result, William, who in the previous two years had become a more outgoing, happy, relaxed and confident young man, went back into his shell, cutting himself off, spending hours at a time alone in his room or going for walks alone with his portable CD player for company. He spent more time with the new loves in his life, Charles's dogs. And now there was no one to whom William could turn, for Tiggy had married and had begun a new life.

Since Camilla's move into Highgrove, much has changed. She has taken over the 'wifely' duties of running a home, taken full command of running Highgrove and, at the same time, has also taken over the task of running Prince Charles's London home, St James's Palace.

According to staff who work at Highgrove and St James's, Camilla has proved to be a most efficient, highly capable, well disciplined and relaxed boss. Both homes run like clockwork. And there is no question that Camilla is the boss.

As one of Charles's valets put it, 'We have been told by the Prince of Wales that Mrs Parker Bowles is now in charge of running the houses and that she now has his full authority to do so. That's it. Nothing more to be said, really.'

To all intents and purposes, Charles

now leaves everything to Camilla to sort out. To that extent, he is much relieved that she has taken that particular, rather irksome, burden off his shoulders.

Officials and staff who flit around the two homes are left in no doubt that Camilla is the boss who must be obeyed. They understand that she has to be consulted on every subject, from dinner menus and flower arrangements to the guests invited to lunches and dinners and the place settings. She also has the additional and more serious task of hiring and firing staff.

Indeed, William has compared his mother's approach to organising royal households and Camilla's more disciplined way. To friends, William laughs and jokes at the totally different approach to life at home now that Camilla runs everything, compared to when his mother ruled the roost.

He accepts that under Camilla's authority the homes run like well-oiled machines, whereas in Diana's days there was a more hectic, wild but more exciting and informal atmosphere which the boys had enjoyed. Sometimes, they used to tease Diana and she didn't mind. Nowadays, life is relaxed at Highgrove but William and Harry don't feel the buzz of excitement and they miss the organised chaos that was so much a part of their life with their mother at Kensington Palace.

William's description some years ago of life at Kensington Palace was revealing: 'Basically, Mummy would let us do anything we wanted, within reason. We could have pillow fights, race around the apartment, watch TV, help ourselves to snacks or a Coke from the kitchen whenever we wanted. If we needed something to eat, we only had to ask the cook. We could do anything we wished. Mummy never said 'No'. There were no restrictions. It was great. We felt totally free to do anything, and we did.'

Recently, William has told friends, 'Camilla's fine. She's nice to Harry and to me and we get along together but she's totally different to Mum.'

He went on, 'In any case, it's now all so much different. Now Camilla's come to live with us, it's no longer the same with Dad as it used to be after Mummy died.'

The tragedy is that William is no longer happy at Highgrove. Staff remember William as a friendly, natural, warm and chatty teenager who always had a smile on his lips and a friendly word for everyone. No more.

William has become more introvert, more private and less sociable. Some even say that William has become 'frosty', hardly speaking to members of the household with whom he used to happily chat away.

The staff find the new William to be less trusting and less communicative. They sense he wants to keep himself to himself, sometimes barely wanting to pass the time of day, whereas before the arrival of Camilla young William would be all smiles, a friendly character, a breath of fresh air around the place.

Before leaving for his hunting expedition in Africa, William told one or two former Eton pals that he was happy to spend as much time as possible away from Highgrove.

During his gap year, William has, in fact, spent little time at Highgrove. He stayed there for much of summer 2000 — June to September — after Camilla had moved in. He then began his adventures around the world.

He has been to Belize with the Welsh Guards for two weeks on a jungle training exercise; spent three months in Patagonia, Chile, with Raleigh International helping local people; and spent nearly four months in southern Africa hunting game. In September 2001, he will be moving to St Andrews, Scotland, to begin his degree in History of Art.

One former Eton pal commented, 'He is happy to be going to St Andrews because Balmoral can now be his weekend retreat. If he had gone to Oxford or Cambridge, then his weekends would probably have been spent at Highgrove. And he didn't want that. He couldn't hack that. This way, William doesn't have to spend much time at Highgrove with Camilla always there.

'It's not that he doesn't like her. He simply feels that she has come between him and his father. He had been so happy with his relationship with his father and that seems to have gone up in smoke.'

Part Two

The Early Years

7

Heir to the Throne

As dusk was falling at the end of a bright summer's day on 21 June 1982, the future King of England, William Arthur Philip Louis, gulped his first breath of air. The little lad weighed 7lb 10oz and had a wisp of fair, blondish hair and clear blue eyes. Doctors pronounced the heir to the throne fit and healthy and William proved it by yelling lustily as his exhausted mother started to breast-feed him.

Prince Charles, who had been at Diana's

side throughout the 16-hour-long labour, was euphoric, phoning his parents, his brothers and sisters and senior staff at Buckingham and Kensington Palaces with the good news. After all, Diana had just ensured that the blood line of the House of Windsor was safe for at least another generation.

Remarkably, only 36 hours after the end of a long and difficult labour, Princess Diana checked herself out of the private wing of St Mary's Hospital in Paddington, London, and stepped into the noise of the waiting crowds, photographers and TV crews. Wrapped in a lace shawl and carried in the proud arms of his father, the yet unnamed heir to the throne slept unperturbed throughout the mayhem of his first photo-call. As the rest of the country celebrated, the exhausted Princess watched proudly as her husband carried her tiny son into a limousine and held him in his arms as they made their way back to Kensington Palace and the beginning of William's life as a vital part of the most famous family in the world.

It took seven days of discussion and

argument before the name of the heir to the throne was officially announced, leading to furious speculation in the newspapers and keen betting at bookmakers. It was known that Diana favoured 'Sloane Ranger' names such as Sebastian and Oliver, while Charles had been holding out for Albert after Queen Victoria's consort. In the end, compromise won the day, with William being seen as a comfortable mixture of the traditional and the trendy.

From the moment Diana realised she was pregnant, both parents were determined to enjoy her pregnancy. Prince Charles read numerous books on the role of fathers during labour and even attended a lecture on childbirth, while Diana herself wore maternity dresses and coats long before her size made it necessary. In all, it was a very public pregnancy, with photographers allowed unprecedented access to the Princess of Wales. In fact, it was probably one of the most talked-about pregnancies in British history, with commentators rushing to explain the historical significance of the royal birth, health writers endlessly pronouncing on the various stages of pregnancy and everyone else speculating on the sex of the unborn child. And it wasn't only in Britain that Diana's pregnancy was closely followed — the United States, Japan, the Commonwealth states and some western European countries all took a keen interest, just as they had at the couple's wedding that had been broadcast live across the world.

Diana always maintained in public that she had no idea whether her first-born would be male or female. In private, however, a scan during the later stages had left her and Charles in no doubt that she was expecting a boy. From the start, Diana was determined to break with the royal traditions that had been carefully outlined to her. Her demand to give birth in a hospital was one which left the royal advisers in a spin. Previously all royal babies, and especially those born as heirs to the throne, had been delivered at Buckingham Palace surrounded by nurses, midwives and doctors in a room specially equipped for the occasion as a labour ward. But Diana was determined that if anything should go wrong with the birth of her baby, then she wanted immediate access to all the latest neo-natal technology. Charles, too, was brought round to her point of view and so William came into the world at a public hospital.

Charles, however, was not so convinced when it came to the choice of nannies for his son. Like many upper-class children, he had been cared for by a nanny from an early age, and for William, he wanted his old nanny, Mabel Anderson, who was well versed in royal protocol. But Diana had her own ideas. She didn't want an old-fashioned, regulated routine for her son. She wanted a nanny who was informal and progressive and who, more importantly, would play second fiddle to her in the nursery. Secretly, Diana did not want anyone to look after her beloved baby: she wanted to do it all herself, but she accepted that she needed help.

She was the Princess of Wales and it was her duty to accompany her husband on many official functions. What she couldn't and wouldn't accept was that she could be superseded in her own child's affection by a hired help. In the end, Charles swallowed his objections and agreed to the appointment of Barbara Barnes, the 42-year-old daughter of a forestry worker, a no-nonsense woman who had no formal training, never wore a uniform and, most importantly, did not regard the royal nursery as her own private kingdom. And she certainly did not see herself as a mother substitute. Barbara was not alone in the nursery for she also had a helper, Olga Powell, an experienced nursery maid. The system worked well. Charles and Diana wandered in and out of the nursery at will, the Prince taking great delight in changing nappies and bathing his tiny son; Diana spent hours talking and playing with her little boy, as well as bottle-feeding him when she had finished breast-feeding him. When William displayed any symptoms of childish illnesses such as a sniffle or a cough, it was Diana who slept beside his cot in the night nursery.

If Diana won the battle of the nannies, it was most definitely her husband who was responsible for choosing the godparents. Diana had wanted at least one of her young friends from her pre-wedding days to be included in the list but it was not to be. It was explained to Diana that the selection of godparents was a tradition that could not be ignored, and that men and women from other royal families and the Establishment must take precedence over anyone she wished to ask.

After much wrangling, and intervention by the Queen, Diana accepted the situation. In the end, the nearest person to her age was Tally, wife of one of England's leading earls, the richest landowner in England, the Duke of Westminster. And Tally was only invited because her husband, Gerald, and Prince Charles were good friends. Otherwise, the list included the former King Constantine of Greece, a close friend of Charles; Lady Susan Hussey, one of the Queen's senior Ladies-in-Waiting; Princess Alexandra; and Lord Mountbatten's grandson, Lord Romsey. The choice which raised the most eyebrows was that of the now-deceased Sir Laurens van der Post, who was 76 at the time but a close friend of Charles's. Sir Laurens, Japanese POW survivor, philosopher, poet and story-teller, was seen as a wildcard entry.

On the afternoon of 4 August 1982, surrounded by members of the Royal Family and his numerous godparents in the music room at Buckingham Palace, Prince William was christened. One by one, the godparents pledged to bring him up in the Christian faith, and to help and guide him throughout his life. As time would show, William would need all the help he could get in the traumatic years ahead.

Both Charles and Diana were determined that William should have a happy and 'normal' childhood, and crucial to this was the decision that the parents would not spend long periods of time away from him. When Charles was a baby he would only see his mother twice a day, once for 30 minutes around 9.00am, and then for a further 30 minutes in the early evening. Otherwise, nannies exclusively cared for Charles for the first five years of his life. Charles also remembered the desolation he felt when his own mother, the Queen, put duty before children and disappeared from his life for months at a time visiting various parts of the world, carrying out her duties as Queen, not only of Great Britain, but also of the Commonwealth of Nations.

With a sense almost of shock, the world witnessed one reunion after the Queen had been away on a royal tour for six long months, when mother and son treated each other formally and politely in that first meeting after so long apart. They seemed almost like strangers meeting for the first time. On that occasion, Charles was told to greet his mother with a handshake. And, as an obedient and dutiful child, that's precisely what happened. There were no kisses or hugs, no laughter and no sense of fun. Charles looked shy and slightly uncomfortable; his mother smiled and shook his hand, permitting herself no spontaneous maternal contact.

Charles had often told Diana of his misery at having to regard his mother as a distant relative whom he was permitted to see only for an hour a day. Diana was determined to have none of it for her child. So when it was time to go to Balmoral for the annual royal summer holiday, the three of them flew together and it was Charles who carried his son off the plane while the nanny walked behind carrying the baby equipment.

Six months later, in January 1983, Charles decided that Diana needed a holiday away from her son. Exhausted from trying to combine the duties of being the wife to the Prince of Wales, attending official functions and all that entailed, constantly feeding, caring and worrying over the needs of young William, Diana's health was causing concern. But the break, a week in Liechtenstein at the castle of Prince Franz Joseph, was not a happy one. Diana spent much of the time in tears, missing William and — some believed — it seemed that she was suffering from post-natal depression. The couple came back to England in the worst of spirits with Diana determined that she would never be parted from William again without very good reason. And, in her opinion, a holiday away from William would never be tolerated while he was still so young.

Her resolve was soon put to the test. A royal tour of Australia for the couple had been announced shortly after William was born, which would take them away from Britain for six weeks. Diana made her feelings clear. Come what may, she was not going to be separated from Prince William at such a crucial stage in his development. The arguments raged between Kensington and Buckingham Palace, with Diana refusing categorically to go on the royal tour without William. Eventually, the Queen agreed that Charles and Diana could take the young prince with them.

Thus, in the spring of 1983, the young family arrived in Australia, complete with Nanny Barnes and a whole host of baby equipment, organic foods, vitamins and food supplements. With his nanny, William was settled in the tiny town of Woomargama in New South Wales, while his mother and father criss-crossed the country. Whenever their schedule permitted, Charles and Diana flew back to spend time with their son. It was another successful break with protocol and, although other trips were made without William, it set the pattern for Diana within the Royal Family. William came first, no matter what royal protocol dictated.

Like his father before him, William was a bright, sometimes precocious little boy. Surrounded by his doting nanny, talked to and played with by his adoring parents, he had an early vocabulary and was naturally curious. During the 1983 summer holiday in Balmoral, when just 15 months old, William was left to his own devices for just a few minutes and spotted a tempting button on the nursery wall. He pushed it, sending an alarm signal to the Aberdeen police headquarters. It wasn't until armed police had raced to Balmoral, sealed off the castle and the entire grounds, that it was discovered that young William had been responsible for the furore. Barbara Barnes was beside herself with embarrassment, while Prince Charles and Diana thought it was all a bit of a hoot.

Like most toddlers, William was into everything. His favourite trick was flushing anything he could get his hands on down the lavatory, including his father's shoes. Like millions of parents before them, Diana and Charles found all this childlike mischief hilariously endearing and instead of chastising the little boy, they nicknamed him 'Wombat' (an Australian small bear). For the time being at least, Prince William was unconditionally adored, unbelievably pampered and the centre of his parents' world.

Then in January 1984, Princess Diana discovered she was pregnant for the second time, and on 15 September 1984, when Prince William was just over two years old, she gave birth to a second son, Prince Henry Charles Albert David, to be known as Harry. And, once again, Diana went to St Mary's Hospital. Like many mothers, fears that William may have feelings of jealousy towards his younger brother had worried Diana throughout her second pregnancy. Sensibly, she consulted friends who had also had young families about the subject and read up on it wherever she could.

Although she was determined to leave the hospital as soon as possible after Harry's birth, she insisted that William must visit them first to establish a bond with the new baby as soon as possible. The morning after Harry was born, William, Prince Charles and Nanny Barnes were driven to St Mary's and taken to see the new arrival. Diana was waiting as they stepped out of the lift. Despite having given birth only 24 hours before, Diana instinctively scooped William into her arms so that she was holding him when he first saw his baby brother.

Any fears that she may have had about William harbouring jealous feelings towards his younger brother were quickly dispelled. In fact, it was an early indication of his caring nature that he took to the little baby in a big way. From the first moment he saw Harry, he was enthralled, wanting to hold him and play with him at every opportunity. In fact, when Harry was christened three months later in St George's Chapel in the grounds of Windsor Castle, William made somewhat of a nuisance of himself when he was told that he couldn't hold his little brother during the photo session that followed. In front of millions of TV viewers, William ran unchecked through the distinguished gathering, even ignoring the Queen as she attempted to reason with her little grandson. There was no doubt that William was becoming what was euphemistically termed 'a bit of a handful', and his behaviour was beginning to ring alarm bells with the Queen and Prince Philip, as well as the disciplined Prince Charles. He had an uphill struggle ahead of him.

Diana, who had worked with children before she married, was completely relaxed with William, thinking nothing of bribing him into good behaviour or laughing at his antics when her in-laws thought she should have shown disapproval. Nanny Barnes, too, doted on her young charge and was often reluctant to adminster the discipline that all young children need.

The signs that something was wrong were piling up thick and fast. Shortly after Harry's christening, the Queen Mother invited the family to Birkhall, her Scottish residence, and Prince William ran riot, apparently, on one occasion, almost destroying the contents of her dining room. He had also earned himself a bad reputation with some of the servants, showing disrespect and being rude to them. From a very young age, Charles had been taught to treat all members of the royal household, including servants and maids, with respect and politeness, but in the family atmosphere of Kensington Palace, Diana had been somewhat lax in teaching William how he must behave. Charles was infuriated with his son's behaviour and insisted that he must be taught good manners and respect to others. Diana sulked, believing that Charles was asking her to be too strict with the young William.

Finally, however, Diana accepted that William was getting out of hand and agreed that something had to be done. She accepted that it was time to stop pampering William's every antic and begin the transition from babyhood to childhood. He was three years old. Charles was all for William following royal tradition and having his early education at home with a governess teaching him the rudiments of reading and writing. But Diana felt that her son would benefit more from mixing with other children, having playmates of his own age. One afternoon, as she was visiting potential kindergartens with William,

she watched as he tried to join in with the
other children. Within a few minutes it
became clear that although William
desperately wanted to join in the fun and
games, he couldn't — because he didn't know
how. That night she told Charles about the sad
little incident and he finally agreed that
William should go to a kindergarten.

As with everything to do with their
beloved son, Charles and Diana thought long
and hard before they decided which school to
send him to. Diana, in particular, was in her
element, researching, asking friends and
relatives and visiting several places, before
finally settling on Mrs Minors' Nursery School
in Notting Hill Gate, a few minutes' drive from
Kensington Palace.

Charles recalled the fuss that had
attended his first day at school and he
desperately wanted to spare William that
ordeal. So, together, he and Diana sat down
and composed a letter to all the national
newspaper editors, asking them to leave
William to attend school in peace. Mrs Minors
spoke to neighbours in the quiet, leafy West

London street, while Diana personally spoke to the parents of every child at the school in a measure designed to prevent leaks to the press, and to apologise beforehand for any inconvenience that William's attendance might cause.

Other precautions were necessary, too. It had only been six years since Earl Mountbatten and others had been murdered by the IRA, blown up in their fishing smack while on holiday in Ireland. No risks could be taken with William, the heir to the throne. Some of the windows in the building had to be replaced with bullet-proof glass, an alarm and panic button had to be installed in William's classroom and provision had to be made for the armed detective who would be with William at all times.

On a sunny September day in 1985, William arrived for his first day at school wearing a pair of red shorts and a checked shirt. He hardly blinked at the phalanx of 150 photographers and television cameramen who had lined up to record the day. In fact, it was his mother Diana who seemed to be the more nervous of the two. It was a friendly, happy school, with three classes of twelve pupils. William spent the first two terms in the Cygnets class, moved up to the Little Swans and finally progressed to the Big Swans. He attended two mornings a week until half-term and then every morning. In this cosy environment, he enjoyed all the games and fun common to most pre-schoolers; finger painting, water play and modelling, as well as learning to count and being introduced to the rudiments of reading and writing.

William acted in two nursery school plays which were attended by Charles and Diana. Baby Harry was taken along, too. He also sang solo. According to royal records kept at Highgrove, 'Prince William was very popular with the other children, and was known for his kindness, sense of fun and quality of thoughtfulness.'

Those are the words written in the official records. But it wasn't quite that plain sailing for the young prince. If Diana and Charles had hoped that William would have some of his less attractive qualities quickly rubbed off him by his schoolmates, they were to be disappointed. A bright little boy, William quickly learned how to pull rank with the other children.

'If you don't do what I want, I'll have you arrested,' was one phrase which could be often heard echoing around the playground. His assigned bodyguard often had to calm down his young charge, but sometimes Wills was too quick for him and a fight would have started in the time it took for the bodyguard to look away. Within weeks, William had been nicknamed 'Basher'.

On another occasion, William pushed even his doting mother too far. One of the children at the kindergarten was having a birthday party and William was playing up badly. He refused to sit down quietly with the other children, and when he was told off he threw his food on to the floor. When he was ordered to pick up the mess, he shouted at the staff, 'When I'm King, I'm going to send all my knights around to kill you.'

When Diana was told of his behaviour at the end of the party, she was extremely embarrassed and not a little angry at her son's high-handed, outrageous behaviour. She told him that if he did such a thing again, he would be punished. But William's unruly behaviour came as no surprise to Diana.

At home, William had by now become quite a handful, demanding and getting his own way, being rude and cheeky to everyone, and refusing to do what either his mother or Nanny Barnes told him to do. He would refuse to go to bed at night, demand that people fetch and carry his toys for him and, on many occasions, Diana would placate her first-born by finding and bringing the toys to him herself. She was desperate to try and conceal William's naughtiness from Charles and the staff at Kensington Palace, though Nanny Barnes and the maids knew full well that he could be quite a handful. He would refuse to put away his toys when asked, refuse to eat his food properly, and refuse to speak respectfully to the staff, which resulted in many stand-off rows between William and his mother.

Generally speaking, however, the little terror would obey his father but only after a minute or so of argument. In principle, both Diana and Charles were against smacking their children but, occasionally, William was given a hard slap on the behind if they thought he had gone too far. And it was nearly always Diana who administered the smack, because the last thing Charles wanted was to smack his children.

Sometimes, even in public, William would misbehave. On one occasion, while watching his father play polo at Windsor Great Park, William went up to a little girl and pushed her to the ground. His mother witnessed the incident, grabbed hold of William and gave him a good hard whack on the backside in full view of the crowd and the photographers. Wills looked at his mother in surprise and anger. But he did do as he was told and apologised to the little girl. It wasn't the first, nor the last, time that William had received a whack from his mother.

But those moments of discipline were few and far between. In reality, both Diana and Nanny Barnes were far too soft with him. Prince Charles, with his strong sense of duty and protocol, and memories of his disciplined upbringing, had begun to worry that his son was running wild and would begin to attract criticism for his behaviour. Charles was particularly embarrassed whenever William caused trouble in public, playing up, being cheeky and disrespectful to others.

It seemed that William's behaviour was particularly unruly when in public, as though he wanted to draw attention to himself. Charles was especially upset by his son's behaviour at the wedding of Sarah Ferguson to Prince Andrew in 1986. Prince William was a page boy, but while the other children were models of good behaviour throughout the ceremony, William was a disaster. He fidgeted throughout the vows, stuck his tongue out at the young bridesmaids and generally behaved like a naughty little boy. This time, the television cameras caught his unruly behaviour and Charles was extremely upset. He continued to try, in the face of some opposition from Diana, to instil a sense of discipline into his little boy, to be consistent in his parenting. But the prince was often away on royal duties and it became obvious that the liberal Nanny Barnes would have to be replaced by someone who would take a stronger line with both William and his younger brother Harry.

At that time — January 1987 — Prince William was ready to move up to his pre-prep school, Wetherby, in Notting Hill, just five minutes from Kensington Palace, and it was decided that Barbara Barnes would take the opportunity to leave. There were in fact two reasons for asking her to leave. One was that Diana had become somewhat jealous of the relationship between Nanny Barnes and William, who seemed to adore her. And Prince Charles believed that Nanny Barnes was too easy going. Charles believed his son, then aged five, needed more discipline and, in January 1987, Barbara Barnes left royal employment to continue her career elsewhere.

Her replacement was Ruth Wallace, a brisk and business-like woman who had worked with sick children before becoming nanny to the family of the ex-King Constantine of Greece, a close friend of Prince Charles

Within weeks, a change was noticed in the behaviour of the two boys as Nanny Roof, as they called her, began to weave her magic. She encouraged them to be friendly to all the servants at Kensington Palace and Highgrove, to play by themselves nicely and, most importantly, instilled in them a sense of routine and much-needed discipline. An important concession was made by Diana. She agreed, after much lobbying by the Prince of Wales, that if Nanny Wallace felt it was deserved, she would be allowed to smack Prince William. But despite her best intentions, Diana still managed to sabotage Nanny Wallace from time to time, often comforting William if he had been punished for being naughty.

A typical day in William's life began at 7.00am, when Ruth would wake him and his brother, wash them, dress them and give them their breakfast at the nursery table. Although their parents were often busy getting ready for public duties, the boys would nearly always see them before each went their separate ways; the boys to school, the parents to work.

Cheekily, William would sometimes salute his father with a giggle when he said goodbye to him. Whenever possible, Diana would drive them herself to school, and always tried to be back at Kensington Palace to read bedtime stories and kiss them goodnight. On Friday afternoons, like many upper-class London families, the Waleses would drive out of town to spend the weekend at their country home, Highgrove House in Gloucestershire.

There, the boys began to love and appreciate the countryside, visiting the farm which was attached to the estate, playing in the trees and riding their little ponies. William, in particular, used to push his new-found freedom to the limit, often disappearing just around bedtime so that he could gain a few precious extra moments of playtime. By and large, however, his behaviour was improving. Somewhat surprisingly, he quickly settled into his new school, despite its heavy emphasis on manners and discipline and William soon learned how to behave in respectable company. He perfected the art of opening doors for women and calling men 'Sir'. He could shake hands like a man and even had his own form of royal wave. Prince Charles and Princess Diana heaved a sigh of relief. At last, their royal heir was beginning to act like one.

Perhaps it was hardly surprising that Prince William had behaved in a rebellious manner. As any armchair psychologist would say, young children who behave badly are often expressing what they cannot say vocally, that all is not well with their world. And all was certainly not well between William's parents. By the end of 1985, his parents' marriage, which had started with such love and mutual admiration, had developed gaping cracks. Diana's eating problems, her bulimia and neurosis, combined with Charles's return to his old love Camilla Parker Bowles had meant that the royal couple were living all but separate lives. And when they were together, the world could see that the atmosphere between them was tense and cold.

By 1987, Charles was spending most of his time at Highgrove. He moved all his personal effects out of Kensington Palace and then moved his entire office, including all his staff, to Highgrove, hardly spending a night in London. Diana, too, was happy that Charles had moved down to the country because she was living the party life in London, enjoying going out on her own and flirting with a variety of men, mainly handsome and single. But she had also begun to show interest in married men. By the time Charles finally moved to Highgrove, Diana was enjoying a passionate, full-blown love affair with Captain James Hewitt of the Life Guards.

The few close friends who knew the royal marriage to be in crisis were not surprised that Charles and Diana had great difficulty living together because their interests were so very different. Despite her upbringing in the heart of the Norfolk countryside, Diana didn't like life in the country, preferring the sophistication, the restaurants, the shops and the buzz of London life. And, just as importantly, all her friends lived in London.

As a result, Wills and Harry only saw their father when they travelled to Highgrove for weekends with their mother. Those weekends, together as a family, should have been special, even precious. But they weren't. William would later remember those weekends as often grim and unhappy, with meals being taken in near silence and there being little of the sense of the fun and games that had characterised their visits in earlier years. Even at that young age, William had sensed very early on that his parents weren't happy together.

He noticed that the relationship between his mother and father was strained, though, by this time, friends realised that the marriage had reached rock bottom. Both Charles and Diana found it difficult to be courteous to each other, let alone have a reasonable, amicable conversation. As a result, during those weekends, Charles would often spend the days alone in his walled garden while Diana, with the help of detectives and household staff, entertained and amused the boys. Charles tried to involve William in gardening, and to that end he bought him a miniature set of garden tools — a fork, trowel and rake — so he could help him, but William showed little inclination towards the activity. It wasn't long before Charles lost his patience and the scheme ended in tears.

Perhaps to compensate for the stuffiness of their father, or perhaps to spite him, Princess Diana began to take the boys on outings to theme parks such as Alton Towers, go-kart racing in Chelsea and even to burger bars. She took William to the theatre to see *Joseph and the Amazing Technicolour Dreamcoat* and to Wimbledon to watch the All England tennis finals from the superb vantage point of the Royal Box.

Even at that young age, William always showed a keen interest in and enthusiasm for all sports, particularly when speed was involved. His father had first introduced William to horse riding at the age of three when William would be walked around a paddock on a leading rein. He soon became tired of riding around at such a snail's pace, and became desperate to trot and canter before he had mastered the art of controlling a pony. But he learned fast under first-class teachers and, as a result, he was quite a competent horseman from the tender age of seven, vaulting on and off his bareback pony with ease and even riding his sturdy Shetland pony standing on the saddle!

It was at Wetherby that William first showed his sporting prowess. He seemed a natural. In his three years at Wetherby he won a number of races and the high jump but his real achievements were in the swimming pool. Much to the delight of his mother, young William proved himself to be a stylish swimmer, appearing in the school gala at the Jubilee Sports Centre, West London. At the age of seven, William won the school's Grunfield Cup awarded to the boy with the best overall swimming style.

But it was not only at sports that William began to shine. From the beginning of his school days at Wetherby, he showed little or no reluctance to come forward, answering questions in class and speaking his mind. He also showed no shyness in singing lessons and speaking out in a classroom play. He sang in the school's Christmas concerts in 1987, 1988 and 1989 and took part in the school play *The Saga of Erik Nobeard or a Viking Nonetheless* in June 1990.

William was really proud that both his parents volunteered to take part in the parents' races held every summer term. In fact, the Wetherby sports day was held at Richmond Athletic Ground which was open to the general public, but the paparazzi never discovered the venue.

William had learned to swim at an early age, urged on by Diana. He used to love accompanying his mother to the swimming pool at Buckingham Palace, as well as to the other pools she frequented in London's health clubs of which she was a member. As Diana commented, 'Sometimes William is more like a fish the way he swims and dives, a natural.'

Much to the delight of his father, William also showed that he loved traditional country sports as much as he enjoyed the thrill and speed of go-karting and skateboarding. From the age of four, when he was taken to watch his first game shoot on the Sandringham Estate, he was hooked. At that first shoot he brandished his toy gun at the sky, at seven he was learning to 'beat' — to drive the pheasants towards the shoot — and by ten he had learned the rudiments of how to be a good shot.

William was becoming something of a rebel as well as a dare-devil, earning a reputation for often getting into scrapes, running into trees, fences, iron bars and lumps of concrete. He also loved climbing tress, the taller the better. Occasionally, his detective had to rescue him, guiding him down from trees 50ft high. He was renowned for constantly hurting himself, though after a few tears he would return to whatever game he had been playing, taking the same risks once again.

Since the age of four, William's favourite games involved making the most of his arsenal of plastic toy guns, rifles, pistols and swords. He was an ace with water pistols, with a reputation for accurately aiming at people, much to their consternation. He also loved teasing women, especially his mother. When he was five years old he developed the naughty habit of pinching her bottom, making her jump. Usually Diana screamed with laughter, encouraging her young son. But then William began pinching other women's bottoms, including maids and servants and visitors to Kensington Palace. Once, he was caught pinching a woman's bottom at the school sports day and Diana had to put her foot down. He was becoming a little menace.

Staff at Highgrove and Kensington Palace, as well as staff working at other royal residences and houses William visited with Diana, were forewarned that young William could be a little horror. Most interpreted his pranks as just that — a mischievous young lad having fun. But sometimes he overstepped the mark.

Diana never forgot the day when William, then five, dug up the remains of a dead rabbit from the compost heap, and swung it around his head while yelling for his mother to look. Diana ran over to remonstrate with William and he threatened to throw it at her if she came any closer.

'Put that down at once,' Diana called to William, but he continued to swing the rabbit around his head, making as if to throw it at her.

'If you throw that thing at me,' yelled Diana, 'I shall be really cross.'

William shouted back something cheeky and Diana moved towards him.

'Don't come any closer,' he yelled, 'or I'll throw it in your face.'

'If you do that,' warned Diana, 'I will tell your father. Do you understand?'

That proved sufficient for, somewhat reluctantly, William threw the rabbit's carcass back on the compost heap.

In 1990, William's time as a day-boy, going to school each morning and coming home every afternoon, was over. Much to Diana's distress, it was time for the little boy to be sent away from home, to become a boarder. But Diana herself had been sent to boarding school as a young girl and she believed that boarding would help William settle down, direct his energies, and encourage him to understand his responsibilities.

Yet again, a great deal of thought and research went into the choice of schools. The home counties of England are renowned for top-quality preparatory schools, many specialising in different areas of excellence. After much research, Diana and Charles settled on Ludgrove Preparatory School in Berkshire. Handy for the road network, reasonably close to both his mother in London and his father in Gloucestershire, the school had a friendly, homely atmosphere with a good record in sport. Most importantly, it was hidden from prying eyes, set in 130 acres, well back from public roads and almost impossible to spy upon. On the first day of the September term in 1990, Prince William, his mother and father mounted the steps of the £2,100-per-term school and shook hands with the headmaster Gerald Barber. On saying their goodbyes, Diana dissolved into tears, while William remained gravely composed. The transition from boy to man had begun.

In truth, his departure to a preparatory school was probably a blessing in disguise. For by the winter of 1990, his parents were engaged in a cold war of such ferocity that those around them were left in no doubt of their mutual hatred. Just about managing to hold their emotions in check for public engagements, the couple would often drive away in the same car, only to split up as soon as they were out of sight and go their separate ways. The media were of course in full flow, speculating endlessly about the true nature of the royal relationship, and while palace officials tried desperately to paper over the cracks, to seasoned observers there was no doubt that this was a marriage in deep trouble.

As in all troubled marriages, it was almost impossible for the children to be kept out of the acrimony — and this one was no different. On a few occasions, William had been witness to some of the screaming matches which occurred whenever the royal couple did manage to get together, usually at Highgrove. After one particularly nasty row, while his mother was sobbing in a locked bathroom, William pushed some tissues under the door with a note saying, 'Don't cry, Mummy'. After another row, he telephoned her favourite restaurant, San Lorenzo, in Beauchamp Place, London, and booked a table for the two of them, to cheer her up.

But despite being away at school, the

pressures of his parents' unhappiness was weighing heavily on him. Other boarders reported to their parents that he would often wonder around the grounds on his own, shoulders hunched and hands in pockets, looking as if the cares of the world were upon him. Even the care that the teachers took to shield William from the news and gossip that was floating around was irrelevant. William knew that his parents couldn't stand the sight of each other, and that made him deeply unhappy.

One incident must have served as a bleak reminder to William just how far apart his parents had become. On 3 June 1991, he was playing golf with friends at the school when one of them accidentally hit him a crashing blow to the head with an iron club. William collapsed to the ground, temporarily knocked unconscious and with blood seeping from the wound. Within minutes of him reaching the casualty department of the Royal Berkshire Hospital, a distraught Diana and Charles were by his side. As doctors examined the wound and pronounced it to be potentially serious, his parents began arguing about the best place to send their son. Charles wanted him to go to the Queen's Medical Centre in Nottingham where he had been treated for a broken arm the previous year, while Diana, accepting the advice of the senior doctor present, insisted that he go to London's Great Ormond Street Hospital for Sick Children. Diana's will prevailed and she sat in the ambulance with William as it raced towards London, accompanied by police cars and motorcycle outriders.

A defeated and chastised Charles followed behind in his Aston Martin sports car. At the London hospital, physicians explained that William had suffered a depressed fracture of the skull and needed an exploratory operation to ascertain the damage. While Diana sat with her son as he came round after the 75-minute operation and stayed by his bedside throughout the night, Prince Charles had to put his royal responsibilities as Prince of Wales above those of being a father. The decision was taken that Diana should remain with William while Charles would continue with his royal duties, which meant sitting through a performance of the opera *Tosca* at Covent Garden. After phoning the hospital to check on William's condition, Charles then boarded a night train to York where he was to discuss green issues with various organisations.

With his zest for life, his cheekiness and his fun-loving personality, William's personality shone through as he careered through his pre-teenage years. By the age of ten, William's manners were impeccable and he had become far more thoughtful towards other people. On one of the Royal Family's visits to Crathie church, near Balmoral, he spontaneously turned to his great-grandmother, the Queen Mother, and assisted her down the aisle of the church and out through the gateway to her waiting car. He then turned to his mother and escorted her to her car. In private, William was also behaving like a young gentleman, standing to attention when spoken to by teachers at school, showing keenness and discipline on the sports field. The days of pulling rank had gone and William only wanted to be treated like every other boy. Indeed, he would go further, sometimes helping younger boys to clean their football boots, and showing them what to do. As a result, he found himself with a growing circle of friends and he loved it.

William was rapidly developing into a natural athlete and becoming something of a golden boy, winning swimming races by metres and showing considerable aptitude at football and tennis. Of course, no one at school had any idea of his other abilities — riding horses, fishing and shooting, go-karting and stalking. Indeed, like his cousin Peter, Princess Anne's son, William was showing all the signs of becoming a seriously good athlete.

Academically, despite some inaccurate and hurtful press reports to the contrary, William was proving his mettle. It became obvious that he was concentrating on his studies and seemingly enjoyed school work. Invariably, he came in the top third of his class at Ludgrove and was always the first to put his hand up for parts in the school plays.

It was at this stage that the caring side of

William's nature became apparent. He felt his darling mother needed his personal care and attention. He had seen her in tears on frequent occasions and he came to believe that he was the one person who could comfort her and stop her crying. He knew that she was frequently unhappy and he hated to see her tears. He saw his role as his mother's protector, making sure she was happy. He was given permission to phone his mother from school each and every night. He also took to writing regular updates about his daily life at school, proudly posting them to her at Kensington Palace. Diana would sometimes drive up from London to pay him visits at school, and the two of them would wander off into the grounds laughing and joking with a closeness that William had apparently rarely experienced with his father. For her part, Diana loved those stolen moments of peace and happiness with her young son.

To those few people who knew Diana well, it seemed as if William had become the one person his mother could rely on for unconditional love and many observers began to worry that she was placing too much pressure on William. She called him 'the man in my life' and in picture after picture of the two of them photographed together, Diana appears to be almost physically leaning on William for support. As the crises in her life loomed ever larger, Diana may have felt she needed all his love and his strength.

Finally, in 1992, after years of tabloid tittle-tattle, the crisis of the royal marriage was brought dramatically into the open, with books detailing the misery of life for Diana in her loveless marriage. To further aggravate the situation, tapes of a conversation between Diana and her friend James Gilbey were published, revealing Diana's bitterness towards the Royal Family whom she believed was deliberately pushing her aside. The tapes also revealed how Diana wanted to be free of them, and free of her husband. Within a few short weeks, all the pretence had been stripped away and the truth of the sham that was the royal marriage was there for the world to see. Throughout the autumn of 1992, as Prince Charles, Princess Diana and the Queen sought to make sense of the highly embarrassing mess, Prince William was left at Ludgrove, to glean what information he could from the few newspapers he could lay his hands on. Doubtless there were the comments and jokes from his school mates to contend with, too. All in all, it was a pretty tough time for the ten-year-old boy.

By December 1992, the Palace had admitted defeat; a reconciliation between the couple was totally out of the question, the royal fairytale was well and truly over. On 9 December, Prime Minister John Major rose to his feet in the House of Commons to read out the statement that the Prince and Princess of Wales would be separating after 11 years of marriage. The day before, a tearful Diana had driven up to Ludgrove to tell her son about what was to come, and to talk through the implications of the end of his parents' marriage. To his eternal credit, the young William responded to this dreadful news with a maturity far beyond his years. He turned to his mother, kissed her on the cheek and said, 'I hope you will both be happier now.'

8

Divided Loyalties

The following day, Prime Minister John Major made a statement to a hushed House of Commons, announcing that the Prince and Princess of Wales were to separate after 11 years of marriage. The only surprise to Members of Parliament, who had crowded into the Commons for the statement, was the Prime Minister's remark that the separation would have 'no constitutional implications' and that Diana could still be crowned Queen. As expected, Mr Major's statement said that the couple's decision to lead separate lives had been reached amicably, that both would continue to carry out public duties, and that both would participate fully in the upbringing of the two young princes.

To William, then ten, and Harry, then eight, enjoying the end-of-term plays and a carol service, the news, of course, did not come as a shock but, nevertheless, William felt miserable and unhappy that his parents were to live apart. In truth, he felt somewhat embarrassed and humiliated that his parents not only wanted to separate but had to announce the fact to the entire world. He couldn't understand why his parents couldn't carry on living as they had done during the last few years, with his mother residing at Kensington Palace and his father at Highgrove; nor could William understand why his parents couldn't keep their private lives private like all his friends at school.

As a result, during that final week at school before the Christmas holidays, William became somewhat introvert, not wanting to mix with the other boys, preferring to keep out of the limelight, for fear he might be teased about his parents' divorce. Of course, the teachers tried to support him, to rekindle his self-confidence, but William remained somewhat subdued and distant.

William confided later that the announcement of the separation had made him feel different, awkward, and even guilty that he was the centre of attention because of his parents' constant bickering. And he didn't like it. No other boys among all his friends had to put up with the embarrassment of having their parents' private lives constantly splashed all over the newspapers. He desperately wanted his parents to stay out of the limelight to spare him the anguish of seeing an article about his parents' private lives filling the front pages whenever he saw a newspaper.

In fact, William and Harry hardly ever saw any newspapers at school — and certainly not the sensational tabloids — because newspapers were banned at Ludgrove in a bid to prevent the two young princes seeing what was being written about their parents. Nevertheless, occasionally the boys did come across tabloid newspapers and, invariably, there would be some salacious, and often inaccurate, story about Charles and Diana on the front page. William would confess later that whenever he saw a tabloid with a picture of either his mother or father on the front page, he would have a sinking feeling in the pit of his stomach for fear of what was being written about them. It was this gnawing antipathy, built up over a number of years, that was partly responsible for William's suspicion of all newspapers, particularly the tabloids.

The separation changed nothing, however, for either William or Harry. As before, they continued to visit their father at Highgrove and, for two weeks of the school holidays, stayed with their mother at Kensington Palace. But Christmas they spent at Sandringham with their father and the rest of the Royal Family. William, however, found Christmas an awkward time, except for the days he spent with his father, and sometimes other members of the family, out in the fields or riding.

William often felt uncomfortable, even claustrophobic, at both Sandringham and Balmoral because he felt he always had to be on his best behaviour in the presence of the Queen and Prince Philip. He noted how his father was always completely respectful towards his mother and knew that he, too, had to behave in the same way, and he found that rather tedious.

Outside, however, he could relax and enjoy himself. He didn't have to watch how he used his knife and fork; he didn't have to remain silent unless someone spoke to him; he didn't have to check that he was dressed correctly for meals. Neither did he have to think how he should address strangers and visitors, maids and footmen, valets and cooks, as well as all the invited dignitaries, such as politicians and their wives, who would come to stay for a few days.

It wasn't that the Queen and Prince Philip didn't show kindness, chat to him in a friendly manner, or make him feel 'at home' at Sandringham or Balmoral. His grandparents did all these things and they would usually smile and be friendly whenever they met, whether at table, in the drawing room or walking around the buildings. And yet William always found himself on the defensive whenever he met them. He wasn't really sure how he should approach them because he noted that everyone else treated them with deep respect and courteous civility at all times, the servants standing to attention and bowing their heads whenever they met the Queen walking along a corridor.

He saw the way his friends greeted their grandparents, giving them a kiss on the cheek and a hug, or giving them a cuddle and a kiss. But neither his grandmother, the Queen, nor his grandfather, Prince Philip, ever kissed or cuddled him or gave him a hug. They would usually just bend down towards him and say a few words and William felt uncomfortable in their presence. It was all so different from life at Kensington Palace, Highgrove or even at school.

For William, life at Kensington Palace with Harry and his mother was so often full of laughter and fun. William loved to run into his mother's bedroom in the morning and give her a cuddle in bed and play with toys, with all of them laughing and shouting at the same time. He used to enjoy the pillow fights with his mother screaming in mock horror whenever he managed to hit her in the face or when Harry would join his mother in the fight against him. Meals were also fun, with no stuffy manners, having to check when it was OK to eat the food in case the Queen hadn't yet started her meal. Such discipline made William nervous and apprehensive. He never felt he could relax in the presence of his grandparents and he didn't like that one bit.

With his mother and Harry, the three of them would just sit down and their food would be brought in for them to eat as quickly as they wanted. When the boys stayed with their mother at Kensington Palace, there was nothing strict about meal times or the need to practise perfect manners, though their mother always insisted they use the napkins provided. And she did always insist that they wash their hands before sitting down to a meal. But it was all fun. Even when William knew he was being cheeky or naughty, Diana would usually just roar with laughter and tell him to be a 'good boy', never giving him a piercing look or reprimanding him.

William felt that even while watching television at Balmoral or Sandringham he had to be on his best behaviour, sitting quietly and correctly on the edge of the sofa, not lying full-length on the floor or on the furniture, with Harry by his side. At home at Kensington Palace, he could eat sweets or chocolate most of the time, though not before meals, but his mother would never let him eat too many at a time. And Diana never minded when they raced around the apartment chasing each other or playing games, often screaming and yelling at each other in their enthusiasm. Occasionally, she would tell them to slow down or keep quiet or go and watch television but always in a gentle, loving way and often with a smile or a laugh.

Indeed, William believed that her sense of fun was one of the great reasons he loved his mother because, sometimes, she would be unable to stop herself laughing. William and

Harry would sometimes attack Diana, tickling her all over her body while she roared with laughter, unable to stop herself as she tried to escape their prying little fingers. William loved those times with his mother and he would never forget them.

William loved spending hours watching Cartoon Network on the television, playing Sonic the Hedgehog, watching action videos with plenty of blazing guns, fast cars and tough heroes. From a young age he was attracted to James Bond movies.

Life with Charles, however, was totally different. William felt in his younger days that his father was rather like a headmaster, telling him how to behave and what to do. His father didn't like him watching television, preferring that his sons read books. William would become exasperated with Charles that he was forever telling Tiggy what the boys should and should not watch on television. He approved of certain programmes, and videos and films which were bought for him to watch.

By the age of seven, William loved watching videos about dinosaurs, other planets, space travel, wild animals and dangerous, poisonous bugs and insects. But William would always go to his father for answers to all the hundreds of questions he came up with, whether they were about geography, wild animals, dinosaurs, other countries or how the stars stayed up in the sky.

As William grew older, however, he came to see another side to his father. He accepted that Charles was in command and that he should never openly be rude to him. But gradually, William discovered his father to be great company when they went outdoors together, particularly at Balmoral. He came to realise that his father was not only very knowledgeable about horses and hunting, shooting and fishing, stalking deer and understanding the countryside, but that he was also a cracking good shot, a first-class rider, and an excellent and talented fisherman. And William came to admire his father's many and varied talents that he had never before appreciated.

As a result, William found himself becoming closer to Charles, hoping that one day he would be as competent at all those outdoor pursuits. And he admired the way his father could make speeches before hundreds of people without being shy or embarrassed and he wondered in his boyish insecurity whether one day he, too, would be able to deliver such speeches with the same confidence.

During the Easter holidays of 1993, however, a few months before William's eleventh birthday, a new person entered his life, someone whom he took little notice of at first but, who, within a matter of a few months, would become his best friend.

Tiggy Legge-Bourke was a young woman whom Prince Charles wanted to help care for his sons when they were staying with him; someone who would become a friend to them, not an au pair exactly but someone they could talk to and confide in. Tiggy would become almost a part of the family, someone who would care for the boys when Charles was away, a sort of surrogate mother. In her inimitable, warm way, Tiggy would eventually become almost a big sister to both boys explaining everything, experiencing all the new things in their life like learning to swim, ride horses, shoot rabbits, ride bicycles and skate boards. Officially, Tiggy Legge-Bourke, who in 1993 was 30 years old, was hired as an assistant to Charles's private secretary, Commander Richard Aylard. In reality, she hardly ever went near the office nor became involved in any official work but became a very modern nanny to William and Harry. She was paid £20,000 a year.

Within a few months, Tiggy had become a wonderful foil for the two boys and William became greatly attached to her, treating her as his best friend, someone he could have fun with and tease. He would playfully fight with her and compete with her, whether it was racing her on foot or on horse-back, climbing trees or skate boarding.

Tiggy, whose real name is Alexandra, was the quintessential upper-class girl, raised in the Welsh mountains on her parents' family estate, Glanusk Park, which occupies 6,000 acres around Crickhowell in Wales. She had first been educated at St David's Convent in Brecon, South Wales, an independent Roman

Catholic school of 150 pupils run by the Ursuline order of nuns. She then moved to the Manor House in Durnford, an élite preparatory school of only 50 girls owned by Lady Tryon, the mother-in-law of Charles's old friend Lady 'Kanga' Tryon. At the age of 13, Tiggy moved to Heathfield, Ascot in Berkshire, one of Britain's top girls' boarding schools, where she enjoyed herself immensely, excelling at netball and tennis. She was also extremely popular though not very academic, attaining only four 'O'-levels. It was ironic that Tiggy completed her education by attending the same exclusive Swiss finishing school as Princess Diana, the Chateau d'Oex, near Gstaad, the Institut Alpin Videmanette. Indeed, Tiggy would become a great companion for William and Harry, for she was not only extremely capable at tennis, lacrosse, netball and fencing, but she was also an outdoor girl, enjoying swimming, riding, hunting, stalking, fishing and skiing.

Before being hired for the job of caring for the royal princes, Tiggy had been trained to look after young boys. After attending a Montessori nursery-teaching course in

London, she opened her own nursery in Battersea, South London, in 1985. It was named 'Mrs Tiggiwinkle' after the famous hedgehog character of Beatrix Potter's children's book which she loved. Tiggy was a natural caring for children, running a nursery, and her school for toddlers became very popular. Three years later, however, Tiggy's school got into financial difficulties and, much to her chagrin, she was forced to close it.

There was another good reason why Charles chose Tiggy as the companion for his sons — she was not exactly a fashion icon, as happy wearing jeans, Wellington boots and a T-shirt and sweater all day, as dressing up in an expensive outfit and high-heeled shoes. And she wore little make-up. Within weeks of taking the job, Tiggy had earned the respect of both William and Harry by teaching them how to shoot rabbits! They had no idea she was such a good shot.

William, Harry and Tiggy enjoyed great times together. And as William grew older, he would try even harder to compete with Tiggy, challenging her at every opportunity. Indeed, when at Highgrove or Balmoral, William would plan their days together, giving himself the opportunity to test his growing skills at her expense. When they first met Tiggy in 1993, William was ten and Harry eight. Both boys loved having an 'older sister' and they would often have mock fights together in their bedrooms or a lounge when they would all scream with laughter and tussle with each other, William and Harry usually teaming up against 'poor' Tiggy. Pillow fights were their favourite, and occasionally they would fight with the scatter cushions on the sofas, hurling them at each other, the boys trying to hit Tiggy full in the face. Each success was greeted with a scream of delight and Tiggy would throw a pillow back at them. They loved it.

Tiggy was no shrinking violet and quite capable of looking after herself with two young lads. Within six months of her arrival, both William and Harry loved their time together with Tiggy because they always had so much fun, whether it was kicking a football around, playing a little 'French' cricket, climbing trees or spending time trying to duck each other during friendly swimming pool fights. She also had a steadying influence on William who, at that time, had been dubbed 'the hooligan prince', for she channelled his enthusiasm and exuberant spirit into a more outdoor, energetic life. Harry adored Tiggy and, the more time William spent with Tiggy, the more he would seek her advice, looking to her for explanations and sometimes confiding in her the thoughts that were troubling him, such as the problems going on in the relationship between his mother and father.

Prince Charles was very happy that Tiggy had agreed to help out, for he appreciated how his sons and Tiggy enjoyed their time together, whether they were lying around on a sofa watching a video or, more than likely, enjoying some outside activity come rain or shine. Tiggy had been asked by Charles to make sure William and Harry enjoyed themselves, but was warned never to spoil them. And he also told her that if there were any problems that arose to make sure she informed him immediately. Charles had always felt guilty that his relationship with Diana had ended in tears and trauma and he was determined to endeavour to shield the boys from the effects of the marriage break-up. To Charles, William and Harry and their upbringing was of paramount importance, far more important than his own happiness. For Charles knew only too well how unhappy and miserable a young boy can feel when brought up in an environment where there was little or no love and affection.

Charles had no need to fear because Tiggy had a sensible head on her shoulders. She didn't spoil the children, deciding, for example, what sweets, biscuits or cakes they were allowed to eat between mealtimes, so unlike their mother who loved to spoil them whenever they were together.

'I know I shouldn't spoil you boys,' Diana would so often tell William and Harry, 'but I can't help it; you're irresistible.'

William enjoyed his time with Tiggy, especially the outdoor activities, but he would become increasingly protective towards his mother. Increasingly, William came to seek Tiggy's advice, no matter what the problem, because he sometimes treated her as a close friend and, he believed, she understood his boyish problems more than either his mother or his father. As a result, William was constantly seeking her advice and, during the next five years, a remarkable relationship developed which would prove invaluable when the moment came when William really needed the comfort, support and love of a woman he admired and trusted.

When the boys weren't staying with their mother, they would nearly always be accompanied by Tiggy whether staying at Highgrove, Balmoral, Sandringham, at Klosters in Switzerland, sailing in the Mediterranean or, sometimes, at weekend house parties to which Charles had been invited. On those occasions, Tiggy would usually be provided with a bedroom next to Wills and Harry but they would be her responsibility, giving Charles the opportunity to relax and enjoy the weekend with his friends.

Such weekends were something of a bore for William because he felt he had to be on his best behaviour. For William, Harry, Prince

Charles and Tiggy their happiest times together were at Balmoral where they would all go out either shooting, fishing, riding or stalking. They would usually take a lunch with them and, whatever the weather, they would spend the entire day outdoors arriving back at the Castle exhausted and frequently muddy, in time for a bath before dinner. William loved those days more and more, though he knew his mother disapproved of shooting and he knew she wasn't at all keen on riding, fishing or stalking. William grew to understand his mother's dislike of such country pursuits and would skate over the details of those activities whenever he phoned her from Balmoral for a chat. Once again, William felt he was only protecting his darling mother from facts she didn't really want to know and she was the last person in the world he wanted to hurt. He had seen her cry too often.

William came to realise that when he and Harry spent weekends with their father and Tiggy, life was much more peaceful and calm than the weekends he recalled with his parents at Highgrove, when tempers flared and voices would be raised in anger. William had always recoiled whenever his parents argued, particularly when the rows reached their peak. He had always sought to calm those situations, wanting his parents to enjoy being with one another, wanting them to be kind to each other. He hated the acrimony that seemed to flare up more and more frequently, and which usually ended with his mother screaming abuse at his father and running off in tears. On those occasions, Wills didn't know what to do. Sometimes he ran after his mother to comfort her, and he recalled the times she would cling to him and hug him while she cried.

But all William could remember about those scenes was the noise, the fighting and the tears. And yet he felt guilty every time his parents rowed with each other. He felt somehow responsible for their tempers and their unhappiness and he didn't know what to do or how he could make them happy. He would say later how he would go to bed at night and cry quietly, fearful that his parents hated each other rather than loved each other. And he cried because he felt useless, unable to help and yet desperately wanting to sort out everything so they could all live happily together.

When staying at Highgrove for the weekend, Tiggy would have all her meals with Charles, William and Harry as if she was a member of the family. At dinner, she would usually share a bottle of wine with Charles and, as the boys grew older, Charles would allow them to enjoy the occasional glass of wine. William liked the fact that the four of them would discuss so many different subjects during mealtimes and that there would be no arguments, no raised voices and no stormy exchanges.

Gradually, over time, however, William came to realise that his mother didn't seem to get on very well with Tiggy and he couldn't understand why. He noted that when he was telling her about some fun he had shared with Tiggy his mother didn't seemed to respond with the usual enthusiasm she displayed when he told her of other incidents in his life. William came to realise that Diana didn't want to hear of the great outdoors life he and Harry enjoyed with Tiggy, riding horses, jumping fences, stalking, fishing, and even shooting. When Tiggy began her job, she would always pop into Kensington Palace for a chat with his mother, but after a few months William noted that Diana had stopped inviting Tiggy into the apartment, preferring her to drop her sons at the door and not come in. This estrangement worried William because he had hoped that his mother and Tiggy would get on really well together, but it was not to be. He wondered why his mother seemed to be jealous of Tiggy, not realising that Diana felt that their nanny was stealing her sons' affection; that her boys were becoming more fond of Tiggy than they were of her. But in William's mind, there was no one who could compare with his mother, no one who could take her place in his life, no one who could take away the love he felt for her.

More than anything, William respected his mother. The more charity work Diana carried out, the more William admired his mother, almost idolising her as he watched people's reactions to her kindness as she moved from one person to another, chatting, smiling to them, holding their hands, reassuring them. He would marvel at the effect Diana's presence had on people she met on visits to hospitals, old people's homes, orphanages, or those afflicted with ailments which kept them housebound or in hospitals or institutions. He would watch the people's eyes, see them light up at her approach and he determined that one day, when he became an adult, he might have the same effect on the less fortunate. But he never believed that he would be able to match his mother's touch of magic that seemed to transform people.

William noted, however, that his father didn't have the same impact on people. He wondered why and he wondered whether, being a man, he would follow in his father's footsteps or would be capable of achieving the same wonderful result as his mother whenever she talked and met people, whether they were men, women or children. Whenever his mother gave William the opportunity to visit sick or disadvantaged people, he would jump at the offer, not only because he wanted to see those less fortunate but also because he simply loved to see his mother's reaction to people and the way those people reacted to her.

When his mother took William and his brother to see teenagers and young people sleeping rough in London, begging for food or money, sleeping in shop doorways or suffering from the effects of drugs, William would be amazed that however rude some of the young unfortunates were to Diana she would, for the most part, win them over. Usually, after an awkward introduction and a few snide remarks, they would chat to her and talk about their problems, believing that Diana, Princess of Wales, was the one person with the power to help them, who would indeed help them, even though she lived in a palace. And why? Because they trusted her. William hoped that when he came to undertake serious charity work, those sick, disabled and unfortunate people would also put their trust in him.

After Prince Charles 'retired' to Highgrove in the mid-1980s, William and Harry looked to other men as father figures. Fortunately, there was no shortage of men willing to come forward and play the role of surrogate father, filling the emotional vacuum left by Charles when he moved his home and his office to Highgrove. Most of the time, William would only see these men for the afternoon but, nevertheless, it meant that male role models were around during the princes' formative years.

Jackie Stewart, the former world champion Grand Prix driver and a close friend of Princess Anne, was one such man. He would take William and Harry to the British Grand Prix, escorting them around the track, introducing them to the top drivers, and answering their hundreds of questions about the cars, the drivers, the track and the art of driving at 200mph. During one visit, William was allowed to sit in the seat of a Grand Prix car while Jackie Stewart explained everything to him. He loved that. King Constantine of Greece, a friend of the royals for many years, is one of William's godfathers and he takes a delight in caring for William, inviting him to his London home in Hampstead for occasional meals. William calls him 'Uncle Tino'.

And there are two 'royals' to whom

William has become very attached in the last few years; Viscount Linley, son of Princess Margaret and Lord Snowdon; and Peter Phillips, the son of Princess Anne and Captain Mark Phillips. David Linley, now in his mid-thirties, a trendy designer and cabinet-maker, likes to ride around London on sleek, powerful motor-bikes and usually dresses in polo-necked sweaters, jeans, biker's boots and black leather jackets. William thinks his uncle David is ultra-cool and the two get on famously together. William has been to his uncle's workshop in Chelsea, ridden pillion on his bike and the two have enjoyed meals out together in the West End.

In David, William found a man young for his years to whom he could speak openly and honestly, who seemed to understand his problems for his parents had also separated and divorced when he was a teenager. In 1991, David Linley accompanied Diana and the two young princes to Austria on one of their first skiing holidays, and he helped introduce them to the demanding sport. One day, when William, then nine, broke down in tears unable to keep up with young Harry, it was David Linley who cheered him up over lunch and persuaded him to have another go. Today, William is a very competent skier and each year loves to accompany his father to Klosters in Switzerland, Charles's favourite ski resort.

And then there is Peter Phillips, now into his twenties, whose parents finally divorced in 1992 after years of wrangling and arguments. Peter is very protective towards both William and Harry for he knows the hell they went through, as he did, whenever his parents argued with each other. Peter Phillips, however, went one step further, becoming William's hero, someone to look up to and admire because he represented Scotland at rugby and lives an independent life. Peter volunteers to join William and Harry when they are holidaying at Balmoral, one reason being that he understands that life at Balmoral can be somewhat boring for young, adventurous, high-spirited boys so he takes them off stalking, fishing and riding. They all get on really well together.

And then, of course, there is the man

who is William's constant companion — his personal detective, the man responsible for his ultimate safety. This man lives with William day and night, knows him better than his own parents, never lets him out of his sight and who is more often than not his closest friend, adviser and confidant. He is the man William turns to whenever the going gets tough.

William's first personal detective was Sergeant Ken Wharfe to whom William became so attached that Princess Diana asked that he should be moved to other duties. Since then, Sergeant Graham Cracker, now 46, a married man with two sons, has taken over and he now spends his life protecting William. Sergeant Cracker sleeps in a room adjoining William's during term time at Eton as he did when William was at Ludgrove.

Sergeant Cracker tries to be as discreet as possible, giving William as much free rein as he needs, desperately trying to remain at a distance from his charge so that he can lead a normal life like all the other boys at Eton. But there is one major problem. Eton is so open to the general public; a public road runs through the school grounds and the boys are permitted a greater freedom than at most British public schools. As a result, Cracker must shadow William whenever he leaves the confines of the college, even for a stroll into Windsor with pals or when he goes rowing on the River Thames. On such occasions, Cracker follows William at a discreet distance and never close enough to hear his conversation. And, of course, Sergeant Cracker will usually drive William wherever he goes or, if there is a chauffeur, Cracker will sit in the front seat, ready for any eventuality. Cracker is, of course, armed on all occasions and at night he literally sleeps with his handgun under the pillow. William likes to drive around in a Range Rover because he finds the vehicle much less pretentious than a car.

For most of the time, William gets on really well with Sergeant Cracker but, on the odd occasion, his presence annoys the young heir to the throne. William was once chatting happily to an 18-year-old girl, but became convinced that Sergeant Cracker could hear their conversation. So William went over to his bodyguard and asked him to move 20 yards away. William was just 13.

But William has been no 'goody-two-shoes'. Indeed, occasionally, quite the opposite. At Ludgrove he quickly earned himself the nickname 'Basher' because he was prone to punching his fellow school pals whenever arguments broke out. Of course, teachers intervened as quickly as possible and the headmaster phoned Prince Charles asking whether he knew of any reason why William appeared to be so aggressive, apparently far more so than any other pupil at the boarding school. Charles couldn't provide any rational answer because William had never revealed such a trait at home. Charles asked the headmaster to deal with the matter in his own way by chatting to William. Within days, apparently, William had understood that he must not simply 'bash' someone for no reason and stopped throwing his weight around.

It was at Ludgrove that William first became overly protective towards young Harry. When Harry joined William at the school, Harry would run to his elder brother for help if he found himself in trouble with his school friends. In an instant William would respond, warning the other youngsters that he would become involved if they dared to tease or bully his younger brother. And because of the reputation William had built up at the school, his warnings were heeded. Such help and assistance forged a strong bond between William and Harry and, as a result, when William moved to Eton in 1995, Harry found life at Ludgrove rather lonely without his big brother for company.

Just as William sought to protect his younger brother at school, from about the age of ten William decided that he should also protect his mother. One day he told Diana, 'When I grow up I'm going to be a policeman.' When she asked him why, William replied, 'So that I can look after you, of course.'

Harry, however, promptly ruined William's chivalrous ambition, remarking, 'You can't be a policeman. You've got to be a king.'

William enjoyed his years at Ludgrove where he did well academically and felt proud when appointed a full monitor in his final year. He only suffered one serious setback at the school and that was during the Easter term in 1993, immediately following his parents' separation, when his school work deteriorated. But, with patience and perseverance, William stuck to his guns and he passed his common entrance examination for Eton with flying colours. His Ludgrove teachers hoped that William would achieve a distinction grade, but he just missed out on that.

Fortunately for the young heir to the throne, William was kept behind a *cordon sanitaire* while at Ludgrove. The press and the paparazzi were forbidden to go anywhere near the Wokingham school in Berkshire. As a result, William, and later Harry, were able to lead remarkably ordinary lives, untroubled by the packs of photographers who would follow Diana whenever she set foot outside Kensington Palace. Such privacy permitted William to live a straightforward existence at Ludgrove, enjoying the same treatment as all his friends without any royal favouritism. William showed himself to be intelligent, kind and popular with his young peers.

Despite his royal background, William

showed no return to his early arrogance or precocious behaviour, never referring to his father or grandmother, never pulling rank. To most of his peers, William was an above-average pupil, a fraction more popular than most other boys. The only real problem he found at Ludgrove was that some of the teachers seemed to treat him as someone 'special' and he didn't like that because it made his friends jealous. More than anything, he wanted to prove himself and not to be treated any differently to any of the other boys. This determination to prove himself meant that William tried really hard at school, but it was on the sports field that William excelled, becoming a hero to many of the younger boys who wanted to emulate this young royal sportsman. It also meant that he became extremely popular.

In 1992 he won the school's Junior Essay Prize which made him feel very proud, but it was on the sports field that William won his spurs throughout his time at the preparatory school. It was at Ludgrove that William learned how to play football, and he fell in love with the game. It was during football games that William once again revealed his aggression, winning 50-50 balls, making hard tackles and becoming quite capable of looking after himself in any mêlèe. In his first term, he was in the winning team of the school's Under-Nine football competition and he represented Ludgrove in the junior swimming team. As soon as he moved into the senior school, he immediately won a place in the swimming team and was a member of a record-breaking freestyle relay team.

Having first won a place in the school's Under-Eleven football team, the following year William graduated to becoming a member of the 3rd XI football team, the Under-12 basketball team and a member of the senior swimming team. During the 1994–95 school year William was appointed Captain of the Ludgrove 2nd XI hockey team and Captain of the 3rd XV rugby team as well as playing in the 2nd XI football team. During his time at Ludgrove, he also won the Cliddesden Salver for Clay Pigeon Shooting, and represented the school at cross-country running and swimming. Later, William received bronze and silver survival awards in swimming and the Swordfish medley skills award.

But it wasn't only on the sports field that William shone. He appeared in Ludgrove's Christmas play in 1990 and took part in the 1993 production of *Christmas Cavalier* by Richard Lloyd. That year he also acted in *The Sword of General Frapp* by John Harris. The following year, he appeared in *Santa and the Vikings*, another Richard Lloyd play. He was also Secretary of the Dramatic Society for the Christmas 1994 production.

In fact, William was keen to be involved in every aspect of the school's activities. He volunteered for sponsored walks for the Wokingham and District Association for the Elderly in both 1994 and 1995.

At Ludgrove in particular, William fought to be treated like any other boy with no privileges. He didn't like the fact that his personal detectives had to keep watch over him day and night. Occasionally, William would deliberately try to lose them. With the help of some friends, they would contrive to make William disappear, hiding him somewhere in the school or in the school grounds. That would cause immediate consternation, particularly amongst his bodyguards, but he didn't seem to care. For a few minutes he was alone, on his own, able to do whatever he wanted without the close attention of one or more detectives. When William and his pals insisted on continuing their disappearing acts, the matter was referred to senior police chiefs who contacted Highgrove.

As a result, Charles went to visit William and asked him to play the game, pointing out that the bodyguards had a job to do and it wasn't fair playing them up and causing them problems when they were only doing their jobs. Charles explained that if anything went wrong, the officers would be in the most serious trouble, and that wasn't fair to them. Reluctantly, William agreed, and his tricks stopped. But William came to detest the fact that he had to be chaperoned 24 hours a day. He was far happier at school when the detectives stayed in the background, out of sight, and a routine was worked out that made it possible for William to feel that he was on his own, while, in fact, the detectives were able to keep an eye on their young charge. William resented the fact that even on holidays overseas he had to be chaperoned every waking moment, and at night he would often discover an armed detective asleep outside the door of his room!

During one skiing holiday, he was tobogganing down a steep hill in the dark, along with other youngsters, and was seen to be careering towards a road at the bottom of the slope, a road on which there was traffic. Seemingly from nowhere, one of the detectives looking after him suddenly appeared, threw himself on the speeding sledge and stopped it only yards before William would have careered into the road. William and the detective ended up in a heap in the snow. The young prince was livid.

'Why do I have to be surrounded by policemen all the time?' he shouted. 'I knew I was safe. Why won't you let me live like a normal person?'

William enjoyed his care-free final year at Ludgrove. He was now a monitor, a member of the school soccer team and had gained a place in Ludgrove's cricket XI during his last summer term. In June 1995, Prince Charles happily agreed to partner William in the school's father-and-son clay pigeon shooting competition which they won quite easily. And the following month, William was thrilled when Diana agreed to partner him in the mother-and-son tennis competition at Ludgrove. Their matches went really well and both Diana and William took the competition most seriously, much to the delight of the hundreds of parents who also attended the sporting event.

It wasn't only tennis and swimming that Diana enjoyed with William and Harry. During *exeat* weekends from Ludgrove, William loved practising his footballing skills at home and Diana would find herself acting as 'goalie' while William and Harry took spot kicks, testing poor Diana to the limit as she struggled to keep a clean sheet against her fast-growing boys. Diana would say later that the boys won every practice match against her, but if it helped their football skills she didn't mind at all. And the boys loved it. Later, William and Harry used to play the same game with Tiggy, whether at Highgrove, Kensington Palace, Sandringham or Balmoral.

And William would really look forward to his *exeat* weekends when he would spend two days and a night with either his father at Highgrove or with his mother at Kensington Palace. The weekends with his father would be quieter, more serious days when they would often go for walks together and William would sometimes help his father in his prized walled garden. They would eat their meals together discussing everything under the sun and William would usually spend Saturday night watching a video.

If Tiggy was at Highgrove, however, the weekends were far more wild, action-packed occasions when he would only see his father for meals while William and Tiggy spent their days outside riding, walking, shooting, playing football or tennis or going swimming. At Kensington Palace life was far more relaxed for

William, alone with his mother. Diana would try to arrange a visit to a museum, art gallery, cinema or amusement park, or organise go-kart racing at which William excelled, showing great daring and skill.

In the summer term, Diana and William would practise tennis at Diana's health club and William would sometimes have lessons with the club professional. William and his mother would sometimes go swimming together and he enjoyed fooling around, ducking her, splashing her and trying to race her. Most of the time, however, Diana, who was a good swimmer, could easily out-swim her son but she often would let him win the races, to encourage him even more.

If William wanted to eat out, Diana might take him to a McDonald's, but William would want to return home if any photographers showed up. But it was with his mother that William showed his teenage interests as he approached his thirteenth birthday. He liked action movies, science-fiction and rock bands like Guns 'n' Roses and Bon Jovi. He liked wearing black jeans, black T-shirts, bomber jackets and trainers, everything that he was not allowed to wear at Ludgrove or when appearing in public with his parents.

As William prepared to leave the protected life of boarding school at Ludgrove for the far more open, challenging society of Eton, however, he showed all the awareness of the tough regime that lay ahead. As he had proved himself at Ludgrove, both on the sports field and academically, now he would need to show his true mettle, proving himself more capable and more competent than the boys he would compete against. He knew that Eton was an élitist establishment, and that the academic standards were high. And yet the brief glimpses of William in those years at preparatory school revealed a young man capable of taking care of himself, and yet with the manners of a young gentleman and the daring and courage of a boy who enjoyed pitting himself against his peers. He would need all those qualities to ensure he succeeded at Eton.

9

Eton Scholar

On 21 June 1995, Prince William became a teenager and, three months later, began life at Eton College, the famous public school on the River Thames at Windsor, founded in 1440 by King Henry VI. Before he arrived at the school in September, however, he had a good idea of what to expect because he had toured the college with his parents during the summer holidays, with the headmaster, John Lewis, a New Zealander, Dr Andrew Gailey, master of Manor House, and the Matron of Manor House,

Elizabeth Heathcote, now in her late fifties and the daughter of an Old Etonian. She has been at the school for nearly thirty years, and is renowned for her kindness, warmth and sense of fun. She was to become the most important woman in William's life for the duration of his years at Eton.

The 'Dame' (as matrons are called at Eton) became William's surrogate mother as she is to all the 50 boys in her care. She is responsible for dealing with all the emotional strains the boys may encounter, particularly in the tough, intensely competitive atmosphere of Eton which William discovered after only a couple of weeks at the illustrious college. Elizabeth Heathcote called William by his first name, as did all the boys and teachers at Eton. All other boys are called by their surnames, but it was decided that it would be better to call William by his first name, as though it was his surname.

On his first day, he was welcomed by Dr Gailey, an Ulsterman in his late thirties, and his wife Shauna, as well as by Elizabeth Heathcote. He was shown to his room, a small study-cum-bedroom which would be his 'quarters' for his five-year stay at Eton. His sole privilege was his own private bathroom, whereas all the other 49 boys in Manor House, a four-storey, ivy-clad building, have to share bathrooms.

Dame Elizabeth, however, is the steady rock to whom all the boys turn for advice, sitting at lunch and dinner with the younger boys in the House while Dr Gailey sits with the older boys. Dame Elizabeth dishes out medicines and aspirins, signs 'chits' enabling the boys to buy on tick essential items like toothpaste, socks and stationery from local shops, billing parents at the end of each term. Above all, however, Dame Elizabeth would listen to any problems the boys might have, watch for any incidence of bullying, provide a shoulder to cry on, and act as an adviser helping the younger boys to settle into the unusual lifestyle of Eton College. Most weeks, Dame Elizabeth will invite a group of boys to her apartment to watch television, discuss some aspect of life at Eton and most Saturdays she holds coffee parties after lunch.

During that first term, Dr Gailey would sometimes knock on William's study door, dropping in for a chat, checking how he was settling in, coping with everything, and enjoying his new life. His wife would also invite some of the boys to her rooms for tea as they monitored the atmosphere in the House, encouraging the boys to enjoy living together in each other's pockets, eating their meals together, attending lessons together, and negotiating the mundane details of communal life.

Like every other boy at Eton, William was assigned his own personal tutor, Mr Stuart-Clarke, a young English teacher, who was charged with maintaining a continuous supervision over William's academic performance and intellectual development. For two hours each week, William would report to his tutor's rooms, chatting about his school work, his sporting interests and his relationships with other boys in the House. It was during these chats that William's 'order cards' — report forms — on which his teachers record his effort and attainment in class at three-weekly intervals, would be discussed. William was also invited to Mr Stuart-Clarke's home for informal evening meetings twice a week, more often than not with other boys, where they would all chat together over a mug of coffee or a cool soft drink.

Perhaps because of his successful years at Ludgrove, William did not find his early weeks at Eton as daunting or traumatic as many other boys in the House. He seems to have been well prepared for the rigours and idiosyncracies of Eton life. But, like every other new boy, he was somewhat taken aback by some of the strange ways at Eton.

Eton College is so very different from all other boarding schools and, to a great extent, is quite different from most British public schools with its traditions and protocol. It seems that Eton teaches most subjects under the sun including Latin, classical Greek, Arabic, Mandarin, Chinese and Japanese, as well as the modern European languages. But lessons are also provided in other subjects such as art, music, computer studies, cookery and even car maintenance.

William chose to play soccer and to row, but Etonians can also play rugby, cricket, tennis, fives and racquets as well as the famous Eton Wall Game, held once a year, in which a wall is defended while others attack. There has been no score in this extraordinarily peculiar game for decades!

The uniform at Eton is like no other in any British public school. The boys wear black tail-coats, a waistcoat, pinstriped trousers and a stiff white collar every day. When they walk into nearby Windsor, however, they are allowed to wear ordinary, casual clothes. William was one among 1,260 boys (there are no girls at Eton), who live in 24 houses accommodating about 50 boys each. Fees are around £14,000 a year, but extras bring that total to around £16,000. Eton used to be regarded as an élitist school, filled with plummy-voiced sons of the aristocracy, the upper classes, land-owners, bankers and Tory grandees. To a great extent, all that has changed during the past 20 years and now Eton society is far more egalitarian. In the past decade, Eton has set its reputation on academia rather than snobbery. Until 1990, parents had to put down their son's name almost at birth to ensure entry to the college, but this has since changed. Nowadays, places will only be promised when the child reaches 11 years of age and then only if they pass the tough common entrance examination. Even William would, allegedly, have been turned down for Eton if he hadn't passed the exam, but fortunately he did rather well.

One of the reasons why Eton was chosen by both Charles and Diana was because of the college's unique education system as well as being noteworthy for the close camaraderie enjoyed by the boys. Charles hated the years he spent at Gordonstoun, in Scotland, with a passion and he didn't find a single friend there with whom he kept in touch after leaving. At Gordonstoun, Charles felt bullied, estranged and isolated, and later referred to that period of his life as being 'like a prison sentence'. Eton, on the other hand, is renowned for creating a friendly, family atmosphere as well as moulding the students' characters for life. There exists at Eton a unique pastoral care system, a complex network of people and informal relationships designed to ensure that no one slips through the net and no one's troubles go unnoticed.

In Manor House, as in all of Eton's houses, the housemaster is always chatting to boys around the House, his wife always attentive to any problems and, of course, Dame Elizabeth, who dishes out the aspirins, is usually the first person to whom a boy is likely to pour out his heart. As a result, the great majority of boys find that the friendships they forge at Eton often last a lifetime. That is extremely important for William because it is unlikely there will be other opportunities for him to forge strong friendships once he leaves the college for his life is likely to be ordered, if not pre-ordained, and restricted by protocol and tradition.

From his first weeks at Eton, William found a wonderfully ordered life, so very different from the existence he had been living, having to divide his time between school and one or other of his parents. During the holidays he would usually spend weekdays with his mother and weekends at Highgrove with his father. Life in Kensington Palace was a world apart from life at Highgrove. William was never sure which one he preferred. For example, at Kensington Palace William would dress all day in a baseball cap, a shirt and jeans; at Highgrove, he would dress in old clothes for messing around during the day and more formal wear for dinner at night; and at Balmoral, he would dress in a kilt!

From William's perspective, however, he discovered he wasn't the only privileged schoolboy at Eton. His grandmother might live in a palace; his father might be the heir to the throne; his mother might be considered the most glamorous woman of the age; but Eton also educates other boys whose parents live in palatial surroundings, own two or three homes in various parts of the world, fly around in their own planes and helicopters, and have their own servants and chauffeurs. Indeed, some boys could also boast of royal parentage. Like William, a few of the boys even have their own bodyguards. And William also discovered over time that he wasn't the only boy at Eton who had had to live through the trauma of divorcing parents, although no other boys had to endure such a public marital split with graphic daily newspaper reports of the state of their marriage and the other parties involved.

Prince Charles and Diana hoped that Eton would give William an air of self-assurance, an in-built confidence, something which both Charles and Diana singularly lacked at the completion of their education. And so it has proved. William has not only thoroughly enjoyed his schooldays at Eton but has also done remarkably well academically and showed great prowess in his sporting activities. He has also built up a coterie of close friends to whom he will be able to turn for advice, friendship, camaraderie and fun in the years to come.

Of course, William had to be guarded 24 hours a day by detectives during the years he was at Eton because the entire college is easily accessible by public roads, creating major headaches for those involved in organising his security. At Fortress Ludgrove, as his former school was known, the school buildings were less accessible, set back from public thoroughfares, and virtually impossible to penetrate without breaking trespass laws. As a result, William's and Harry's bodyguards at Ludgrove were able to give the royal children a great deal of space, and the detectives remained unobtrusive most of the time. Eton, however, proved a far more difficult proposition. Indeed, the senior Royal Protection Squad officers who surveyed the college before William joined the school declared the job to be 'a nightmare', for the entire school is so open and virtually impossible to police with just one or two armed men.

William had hoped that he would not require constant surveillance at Eton because he would always be amongst a group of young men, difficult to pick out or harass. But although, initially, he raised a mild objection to their presence, he quickly agreed that a constant guard would be necessary after his father pointed out possible scenarios if there were no armed bodyguards. Come what may, William had to accept his constant close companions and decided to make as little fuss as possible to make his life more pleasant and the job of his bodyguards as convivial and easy as possible. It was after his chat with Charles that William came to realise that after Eton he would never again enjoy such freedom of movement, freedom to strike up friendships with whoever he wanted, freedom to come and go without hindrance.

And yet, whenever William left the confines of the school or Manor House to walk into Windsor for tea or to shop, usually accompanied by two or three school chums, two armed detectives would always follow. They would be dressed in smart suits, usually looking like businessmen, but in their shoulder holsters they were carrying Heckler & Koch machine pistols. The two bodyguards would always keep William in view, usually walking between 20 to 50 yards behind him. If the town was crowded with shoppers, or as often occurred during the summer months, with thousands of tourists, the detectives would cover William more closely, only permitting the heir to the throne to walk ten yards ahead.

For his part, William would take no notice of the two men but some of his friends found the experience somewhat eerie initially. His good friends, however, soon grew to take as little notice of the armed guard as William.

For the most part, William retained his anonymity while walking around Windsor with his pals. Of course, he looked no different from any other young Eton scholar out for the afternoon, but as he grew older and his looks became more recognisable and well-known, more townspeople would have a second glance at the handsome, fair-haired, 6ft tall young man with the ready smile and realise that the young man was indeed William, the son of the adorable Diana, Princess of Wales. Some local people would pass him and say 'Good luck' in a quiet voice so as not to attract attention. William would usually reply with a 'Thank you' and keep on walking, for he had been advised by his bodyguards not to stop and talk to anyone on such occasions.

Tourists, however, became more adventurous as William's sixteenth birthday loomed and he became that much more recognisable. During his first summer at Eton — 1996 — William was still very much a boy and, to strangers, no different from the hundreds of other young Etonians they saw out and about. Consequently, tourists from abroad and visitors to the town, who only had a sketchy idea of what young William looked like in the flesh, barely had a clue as to William's identity.

By the summer of 1998, however, photographs of William taken at his mother's funeral and during his visit to Canada, showed how the young prince had suddenly blossomed into a well-built, tall, young man, so very like his mother, and now he was far more easily identified by those who visited Windsor in the hope of seeing him. Those tourists who did recognise William during that summer term, however, only wanted to look at him rather than speak to him. Some would simply stare at him as he walked along the road, others would point to him, showing other people in their group which boy William was. But, for the greater part, they were loath to approach him and speak to him, seemingly fearful that they might be intruding on private grief. In that way they showed respect for William's privacy and the memory of his mother for which William was very grateful.

In the summer term of 2000, however, William would walk around Windsor looking down at the ground, his head bowed, because he was so tall — at 6ft 3in — and so easily recognisable that it was necessary for him to take this evasive action to prevent tourists taking liberties with him. William did all he could to conceal his identity, often walking a couple of paces behind his school chums so that visitors to Windsor couldn't identify him. He would remain calm throughout those visits to Windsor and only react when people began taking photographs of him in the street as though they had a right to do so, simply because he was the heir to the throne or because he was his mother's son. Nothing enraged William more than people taking photographs of him.

Instinctively, William would react by ducking his head so that people couldn't get photographs of his face. William would just keep walking but would do all in his power to frustrate the visitors, or whoever, getting the photograph they wanted. He didn't see what right they had to take photographs of him without permission, as though he was simply there for their benefit. His annoyance stemmed from the countless times he had seen his poor mother return to Kensington Palace, tearful, miserable and sometimes angry, simply because of the disgraceful antics of the scrum of paparazzi photographers who had chased and hounded her for their personal gain.

While still a young boy, William had come to the conclusion that many paparazzi photographers chased and harassed his mother in a deliberate attempt to upset her, anger her, and reduce her to tears. They knew such photographs would earn a far greater fee with the tabloid editors and the sensational overseas newspapers and magazines if they could produce pictures of Diana angry, unhappy and tearful. It was this understandable antipathy towards paparazzi photographers that led William to do all in his power to thwart the paparazzi as much as possible. Before the age of 12 William had vowed never to show that he was upset with what he considered to be the underhand, spiteful and repellent antics of those photographers.

In private, William would tell his pals at Eton that on occasions he would dearly and happily love to thump any of the paparazzi photographers who had made his mother's life so wretched. On one occasion, three of his Eton school friends offered to 'fill in' one persistent paparazzi photographer who seemed to spend most of his time waiting on street corners for William to walk by. William, however, asked them not to take any such action against photographers because it would only lead to trouble.

During his childhood years, William didn't mind photo sessions, when a selected few photographers would be invited to take pictures of Charles, Diana and young William. On one occasion, when he could barely walk, William was quite taken by a television camera, going up to the camera and examining it in some detail while the poor cameraman did all in his power to keep the young royal in focus. But William came right up to the lens, looking at it from a few inches, causing much laughter and merriment from the royals and everyone else attending the photo session. The occasion also prompted many smiles around the country when William's antics were shown on television that evening.

During his early years, he didn't seem to mind when television cameramen and photographers took pictures of him and Diana walking along, attending polo at Windsor Great Park or at other functions Diana attended. It was only when he realised to what extent photographers hounded, frightened and upset his mother that William developed a deep suspicion of cameramen which continues to this day.

When William went skiing with Harry and his mother at Lech in 1995, he took on the role of protector, despite the fact that all three had armed bodyguards with them and their own detectives. But William noticed that, having agreed to take no more shots of his mother that day, a group of photographers had ignored the agreement and began to tail her down the slopes. Willliam, a good skier for his age, immediately went over to the group and remonstrated with them, threatening to take away their cameras if they didn't leave his mother alone. The photographers were somewhat taken aback by William's reaction and the situation was only calmed after William's personal detective skied over in an effort to defuse the situation. But William was adamant and won the argument. The detective did succeed in securing a promise from the photograhers that they would go away and leave the royal party in peace.

William has learned from a remarkably young age that there is no *quid pro quo* with the paparazzi or the tabloid press. He firmly believes, according to a theory based on first-hand knowledge, that if an agreement is made to pose for a few pictures in return for being left alone for the rest of the day, the photographers will not abide by the agreement. He has found that, more often than not, they will still tail, shoot film, aggravate and invade the privacy of the royals if they think they can get away with it. It doesn't matter if such agreements are reached on holiday, on a ski slope, or a beach or while visiting a theme park, for William is convinced that the Royal Family should never trust photographers or the press.

As a result, William refused to co-operate with photographers, deliberately making their job difficult, and sometimes impossible. For the past eight years, William has frequently made life difficult for photographers even during photo-calls which had been arranged weeks before. He has on occasions refused to keep to photo-call agreements which had been made weeks earlier by staff who work directly for the Prince of Wales. In his way, William goes out of his way to be deliberately awkward, teasing them, paying them back in any possible way for the misery their colleagues put Diana through on a daily basis.

Deliberately, William will be non-committal and unco-operative towards photographers, fully aware that he is causing them problems. He simply doesn't want to go along with anything that the press wants to organise as a form of retaliation for their previous treatment of his mother. Even today, despite the fact he is 18 years of age, William can still become sulky and unco-operative whenever he has to attend photo- shoots. He doesn't necessarily understand why he should have to take part in such private photo-calls, such as enjoying summer or winter holidays or fishing in the River Dee at Balmoral. He simply believes that the photographers are invading his privacy, and finds it difficult to accept that he has a duty to pose on such occasions.

During one famous photo-call on the banks of the River Dee at Balmoral, with his father and Harry, William made it very plain that he had no intention of posing for pictures. On that occasion, his father asked him to pose with him, giving him stern, disapproving looks in an effort to persuade him to come and join the photo-call, but William made it very obvious that he was not at all happy. When Prince Charles insisted that he come and pose for the shoot, William obeyed, but most reluctantly and, as a result, the photographs the pressmen sent back to their offices were of poor quality. Superficially, the photo-call on the banks of the Dee appeared to show William as a cheerful, gangly youth with a ready smile. The reality was that only a handful of frames from countless rolls of film shot by the assembled photographers showed what everyone wanted to see. The rest, left on the dark-room floor, showed endless images of a gloomy William staring listlessly at his shoes; a sullen, unco-operative William wishing he was anywhere else; an unhappy William deliberately ignoring his father's coaxing to put on a happy face. Only the promise that he would be left alone in peace to enjoy the rest of his holiday at Balmoral finally persuaded him to co-operate. But his compliance was still grudging. Only twice did he briefly lift his head up to look directly at the cameras.

But William's obvious displeasure was, unfortunately, faithfully reported by the assembled newsmen, the royal correspondents writing reams of copy about the 'unhappy' heir to the throne. On the face of it, the general public believed that William was simply not enjoying his fishing holiday with his father, rather than William being deliberately negative towards the press as a result of their treatment of his mother. William's behaviour on that occasion caused child psychologists to wonder why he had reacted so negatively.

Their conclusions led to the worst case scenario. Most considered that the damage Charles and Diana had inflicted on their elder son through their lack of self-control was nothing short of catastrophic. They believed that Diana's *Panorama* confession and Charles's Jonathan Dimbleby interview had been disastrous for the teenage William, suggesting to the world that both his parents were untrustworthy and deceitful. Others believed that Diana's confession revealing details of her own sexuality and adultery, talking to the nation of such personal, intimate and delicate matters caused the young, vulnerable, pubescent William shame and humiliation. The psychologists believed that as a result of his parents' behaviour, William found every newspaper article about his mother or his father excruciatingly embarrassing.

In 1994, William was even reduced to tears when his father ordered him to pose for a group holiday photograph when enjoying a Mediterranean holiday on board the yacht *Alexander*, owned by the millionaire John Latsis, who has been a friend of the Royal Family for decades. On that occasion William slipped away as the group of holiday-makers took up their positions for the photo-call, but his presence was missed and Charles had to coerce his son into the happy family portrait. William was obviously deeply upset at having to obey that order and began to cry. He could be seen desperately trying to brush away his tears as he finally obeyed his father and walked back to the group. But he was still determined never to pose again during that holiday, revealing the stubborn streak in his nature.

William's depth of feeling towards the paparazzi was not surprising. Not only had he witnessed the treatment meted out to his mother by photographers ever since he could remember, but he had also suffered at their hands. In the summer of 1996, Diana had booked a villa in the South of France where she intended to holiday with William and Harry and, of course, their accompanying private detectives. Unfortunately, the villa could be seen from woods not 200 yards away, affording a vantage point from which the family could be put under constant surveillance by photographers.

As a result, the family holiday was ruined. The paparazzi discovered their hideaway villa and all but camped out in the wood. Night and day, relays of photographers from various photo agencies kept a vigil. Neither Diana, William nor Harry could venture out on to the terrace or to the swimming pool without the photographers snapping away in delight. Diana's detectives tried to persuade the photographers to leave the family alone but they refused, saying they were only doing their jobs. In fact, there was nothing the detectives could do because the photographers were on public land.

William, however, became furious at the intrusion and could not understand why the photographers could not be sent packing. He appealed to his mother to do whatever was necessary to get rid of the paparazzi. But she knew from years of experience that nothing could be done to send them packing, except by asking as politely as possible. And that they refused to do. As a result, William decided to play hard-ball. He refused to go out during daylight hours, so determined had he become to thwart the paparazzi encamped on the hill above them. Harry didn't appear to mind the presence of the photographers and enjoyed his holiday, but he didn't like the fact that his older brother refused to leave the confines of the villa during the day. As a result of William's persistently dark mood, Diana decided to cut short the holiday, so they quit the villa and returned to London.

It was because of such awful experiences that William continued his complete disdain for the press in general and photographers in particular. Of course, for much of the time after the troubles in his parents' marriage hit the headlines in 1990, newspapers were deliberately kept away from William and Harry to protect their sensibilities. At Ludgrove, for example, when the boys attended away football matches, the coach driver would take circuitous routes in a deliberate attempt to avoid newsagents who might have billboards outside their shops with headlines about the latest royal scandal. At Ludgrove, newspapers were heavily censored for the same reason and the tabloids banned. Indeed, at Kensington Palace, Highgrove and Balmoral, newspapers were kept in the background in an effort to protect William and Harry from the gory details of their parents' break-up.

During William's last summer holiday with his mother in July 1997, at Castel Sainte Terese, Mohamed Al Fayed's villa in St Tropez in the South of France, the royal party were able to enjoy their two-week break with little interference from the paparazzi. No photographers were able to get near the Fayed villa. But when Diana, William and Harry ventured out to a beach or boarded Fayed's magnificent yacht, *Jonikal*, boatloads of reporters and photographers would close in on the royal party. Photographers armed with long-range lenses and reporters with high-powered binoculars caused some distress, particularly to William. Once again, he became angry and frustrated that the family could not enjoy a few hours by themselves without the press intruding on their private life. That was the reason why, on one occasion, Diana took it upon herself to take a fast speed-boat to the reporters and photographers to plead with them to move away and leave the family in peace. They ignored the plea and, as a result, the family returned to the sanctuary of the villa. It was just another episode William would never forget.

William, however, is not always so antagonistic towards photographers. He accepts that, as the heir to the throne, the public do have a right to see official photographs of him and his family and, by tradition, photo-calls are arranged for such events. On some occasions, he happily co-operates. It is when the paparazzi try to invade his privacy or that of his family that he becomes very, very unhappy and memories of his mother return to haunt him. He has difficulty coping with that. And understandably so. For example, William was prepared to pose happily for the necessary photograph at his confirmation at Windsor Castle in March 1997 when, with Diana and Harry, they sat smiling while a phalanx of photographers clicked away. But those occasions would be few and far between.

Even when he was much younger, William didn't appear to relish the idea of posing for pictures. During the Waleses' official royal tour of Canada in October 1991, Prince William, then only nine years old, didn't fancy posing for the official photo of the Royal Family with the crew of the Royal Yacht *Britannia* leaving for home. Instead of posing quietly, William decided to wave at the crowds on the quay below. His mother told him to keep still and stop waving, but William took not the slightest notice. So Diana slapped his arm quite hard, telling him, 'Do as you are told.' The naughty William, however, continued to wave, earning himself another whack on the arm from Diana. Young William then went into a sulk. A few minutes later, the

Royal Family should all have been together on the top deck waving goodbye to the massed crowds. William, however, had vanished. Charles disappeared from view, took hold of his son and told him to join the others immediately on the top deck. A reluctant William walked sheepishly back to join the others, barely smiled and hardly managed a wave.

Many psychologists, however, do believe that William's behaviour stems from the fact that he was scarred by the break-up of his parents' marriage and also by the public revelations of intimate details of their respective lives. Some believe that before the death of Diana, William was showing signs of being a 'damaged' youngster, walking around with his head bowed, hiding his face from the cameras, giving the impression that he fears the instrusion of the camera into his innermost thoughts. Some believe William to be deeply suspicious of strangers, sometimes behaving like a hunted animal when he's not surrounded by close friends or his immediate family.

The psychologists believe this because of some of William's reactions when simply seeing photographers. The press reported in July 1997 that William was being driven by his father to watch a polo match at Windsor Great Park when he saw cameramen waiting to photograph them. To thwart them, he immediately dived on the floor of the Aston Martin, ensuring that the photographers would not be able to capture a single frame of him. It is such instant reactions that suggest to the psychologists that there must be deep reasons for William's behaviour.

While many prepossessing, handsome teenage boys rebel by trying to be different from their peers, William prefers to bury himself in a crowd and yearns to remain anonymous. That is the principal reason why William was so happy at Eton. All the boys, including William, wore the same uniforms, attended the same classes, played the same games, and William was treated in exactly the same way as all the other teenage boys. He felt protected at Eton, cut off from the outside world, shielded from the glare of publicity, providing him with the stability he needed and the anonymity he craved.

10

Diana's Legacy

Throughout his teenage years, William was greatly influenced by his mother who was desperately keen for him and his younger brother to grow up like normal, ordinary kids, experiencing as many facets of life as any other teenager. That was the reason Diana was seen dressing her boys in jeans, sneakers, T-shirts, bomber jackets and baseball caps, taking them to cinemas and go-karting, visiting burger bars and taking them on skiing and summer holidays.

That was also the reason why Diana was happy for William to attend typical upper-crust teenage parties, including the more risqué, wild dances for boys and nubile pubescent girls. It was also the reason Diana took her sons to see the other side of life in '90s London. Together, they visited the homeless to see how young people struggled to survive in the cold, harsh, unloving world. They talked to the disadvantaged and listened to their real-life stories of broken families and desperate loneliness; they chatted to teenage girls and boys who were experiencing bleak times, thrown out of their homes, living rough in London, trying to survive on a few pounds a week, begging in the streets and surviving on hand-outs and soup kitchens. And Diana also took her sons to visit and talk to those youngsters in real trouble, many of whom were drug addicts, while others, both boys and girls, had taken to prostitution or drug abuse — often both — in their battle for survival.

Diana had shown William how fortunate he was to be living such a privileged life. There was also another reason which Diana would explain to William. She told him how she hoped that he would follow in her footsteps, showing care and understanding to those less fortunate and treating them with respect, gentleness and empathy. William admired his mother for teaching and showing him the darker side of life, a life that he would never know and would have difficulty in fully understanding. But he did vow to follow in her footsteps and try to help those much less fortunate than himself.

Princess Diana wanted to show William a facet of life that virtually no other members of the Royal Family had ever experienced. It was a criticism that Diana occasionally levelled at the Royal Family, and her criticism included the Queen, Prince Philip, Charles and his brothers. Diana had been angry and frustrated when the Royal Family, backed by the Establishment in the form of senior royal courtiers, tried to prevent her becoming closely involved in helping AIDS sufferers. She was determined to bring their plight to public awareness and treat them like ordinary people suffering a terrible, debilitating illness and not like the 'unclean', to be ignored. Diana's determination to promote AIDS charities, in fact, won her admiration around the world and showed the Royal Family that their instinct to ignore AIDS sufferers was not only wrong but ill-conceived.

To her credit, Diana never levelled the same accusation at Princess Anne. Though the two women never got on well together, didn't like being in the same room and could barely hold a polite conversation, Diana always respected Anne. Diana knew the prodigious amount of effort Anne put in to the Save the Children charity, which included hands-on involvement in the most deprived and poverty-stricken areas of Africa. And Diana also respected Anne because she sought no publicity for herself, only for the charity and the youngsters in need.

Diana would explain to William that although he would have to conform to royal tradition and carry out the necessary duties throughout his life because it was his lot to have been born into the Royal Family, he didn't have to always conform to protocol, convention and tradition. She wanted William to think independently, to make his own decisions and not to be bound solely by the strictures of life within the Royal Family.

And she would tell William how she had fought against some of the petty strictures members of the Royal Household and Prince Philip had tried to impose on her. Diana had frequently bucked the system and done her own thing. Sometimes she had won the battle and protested to such a degree that she had been permitted to deviate from royal traditions and go her own way. But that wasn't the case very often.

From the very first months of her marriage in July 1981, Diana had shown a disdain for the royal way of doing things. She had fired many of Charles's staff, and demanded she live the life she wanted without the restrictions the Establishment imposed. She had decided to have her first-born delivered in a modern London hospital and not, as tradition dictated, in a room at Buckingham Palace. And from the first she made all the decisions: breast-feeding her own children which went against royal tradition; and insisting on naming her children herself rather than permitting the Royal Family to dictate to her. And she didn't simply let nanny take over looking after William and Harry, insisting on doing many of the maternal jobs herself. Diana loved bathing and feeding her boys, cuddling and snuggling them in her bed in the morning; even changing nappies delighted her.

Throughout their childhood, Diana was nearly always there for her sons, playing with them, feeding them, encouraging them, hugging and kissing them, so unlike the great majority of royal mothers. And her decision to take lovers and indulge whatever friends she decided upon upset many in the Establishment. Diana took not the slightest notice, even when senior Royal Household officials tried to persuade her otherwise. And, from the moment of her separation in December 1992, Diana became more determined than ever to ensure that her boys grew up to understand and, if possible, experience the lifestyles of their contemporaries from as many different social backgrounds as possible; such attitudes were an anathema to royal traditionalists.

Diana also decided to introduce her various lovers to William and Harry. She never tried to hide them away from her sons; in fact, rather the opposite, going out of her way to get them together, to involve her sons with the men she dated both during and after her marriage. James Hewitt, one of the great loves of her life, became a good friend to young William.

Diana and Hewitt first became friends in 1983, when William was just 18 months old, and she and the handsome cavalry officer eventually became lovers. Diana's relationship with the young polo-playing officer blossomed after Hewitt volunteered to give Diana riding lessons in Windsor Great Park. Diana had lost her nerve as a ten-year-old when she was thrown from her pony, breaking an arm. Prince Charles and the Queen tried to encourage her to take up riding again, to rediscover the confidence she had known as a young girl when she excelled at the sport. But to no avail. Seemingly, the only person to instil the necessary confidence was James Hewitt. The daredevil young guards officer would give Diana riding lessons, taking her out in Windsor Great Park and, slowly, Diana regained her confidence and her ability.

As a result, Diana asked Hewitt to coach William, and Hewitt was only too keen to extend his involvement with the family. William had not been too keen on riding when he was very young and Hewitt managed to give him more confidence in the saddle. That helped to win Diana's respect and admiration and brought her closer to Hewitt. Young Harry, on the other hand, needed no such help. A natural, courageous, even daredevil horseman, Harry has a great natural ability. William and Harry would drive down to Windsor with their mother for lessons, while, unknown to the young boys, a strong physical attraction was developing between their mother and James Hewitt.

William and Harry would also meet Hewitt when he called at Kensington Palace for a drink or a meal with Diana, once Charles had moved everything down to Highgrove. The closer Hewitt became to the boys, the more Diana found herself falling in love with the dashing officer. Sometimes, Hewitt would read the boys bedtime stories, play rough and tumble games with them in the drawing room at Kensington Palace and tuck them up in bed. At that time, of course, William had no idea that his mother was having an affair with Hewitt, whom the boys invariably called by his first name, James. But as the months rolled into years, James Hewitt became a constant and regular visitor to the palace and, on occasions, he would phone and chat to the boys asking how they were liking school and enjoying riding, swimming and tennis lessons or whatever. William used to enjoy such conversations with her mother's good friend.

It was only later, when the press revealed that Diana and James Hewitt were lovers, that William began to realise that James — the kind, friendly, fun guy — had become his rival for the affections of his beloved mother. William confessed later that he would watch his mother and Hewitt together, chatting, touching each other, flirting and embracing. William began to notice how much attention his mother gave to James whenever he visited their home, and noticed how long his mother spent on the phone to James rather than playing with him and Harry. And then he discovered that his darling mother used to go away to spend weekends with her friend James. William didn't like that, but he said nothing to his mother.

And after James Hewitt there were others. For the most part, William was totally unaware that his mother became involved with other men. He thought they were just good friends. William met the England rugby captain Will Carling and Oliver Hoare, an expert in Islamic art and antiques, who had been a friend of Prince Charles for many years. Despite his being married to a lovely and beautiful wife, Diane, and the father of three children, Princess Diana fell completely and unashamedly in love with the handsome, sophisticated Oliver. He had tried to help patch up the royal marriage, but the more Diana saw of him the more she became infatuated with him until she found herself hopelessly in love. Oliver Hoare would visit Diana at Kensington Palace in the 1990s, but William and Harry didn't find that in the least strange because the Hoares had often been invited to Kensington Palace for lunch or dinner when Charles was also living there.

As Diana's need for a shoulder to cry on became more desperate, the more Oliver Hoare would be invited to the palace to calm her and help her in her hour of need. The princes became quite used to seeing Oliver Hoare at their home, and he would become another surrogate father to them. Diana's affair with Will Carling, however, was a different matter, for not only was William very happy to see and chat to one of his heroes, the England rugby captain, but he became somewhat starstruck at having such a celebrity as a regular visitor. William was in his element when Carling invited him to train one day with the entire England Rugby XV. William believed that his sporty mother and Carling were just good friends, little realising that they enjoyed a passionate affair.

No one can be sure how William reacted to the comings and goings of his mother's friends and lovers. For the most part, William was at boarding school, enabling his mother to enjoy her affairs in private without either of her sons realising exactly what depth of relationships she enjoyed with the various men who visited their home. And yet William knew, perhaps instinctively, that whenever these callers were visiting, his mother would spend more time chatting to them than concentrating on him and his brother. The very fact of his parents' break-up, separation and divorce caused William great heart-ache and anxiety. It also put him through more emotional trauma than the average break-up because it was such a public affair, the entire nation being informed of every tiny incident on the front pages of the nation's newspapers week in, week out. The publicity never ceased as the couple's relationship bounced from crisis to crisis and it never ceased to bring pain to the young William.

In his lonely bed at boarding school, William would fear for his mother alone in

Kensington Palace, believing that he should be with her to comfort and support her in her hour of need. William had often seen his mother frustrated, angry and tearful, and he would always try to comfort her. At school he felt useless and redundant, and sometimes guilty. He knew that she needed him when the newspapers were being horrid to her, but he couldn't be with her because he was away at school. Frequently, William later confessed that he often felt he was forever in the middle of a tragic tug-of-love between his father and his mother. He hated the cold atmosphere between the two of them whenever they were together. He felt helpless but he wanted to do something to make them both happy. So he reacted by trying to please both.

At first, William took it upon himself to provide the strength that he believed his mother lacked; always wanting to stay with her, protect her, care for her so that she wouldn't need to weep and feel so crestfallen. He would dress as his mother suggested, like all his pals at home on holiday, in jeans and sneakers and T-shirts and baseball cap. He loved going with her and Harry to theme parks, to the cinema, to burger bars, to amusement parks and museums. And one reason he so loved those outings was because those were the times his mother looked happy and cheerful, smiling and laughing with them as they all enjoyed themselves together.

William felt that he was taking over the role of his father who never seemed to visit London, and never stayed at the palace with the rest of the family. But as he matured and became a teenager, William discovered that he also enjoyed his father's company; he looked forward to the privacy of country life around Sandringham and Balmoral where there were no cameras or journalists to ruin his day. There was nothing William enjoyed more than dressing in warm clothes, a Barbour and hiking boots and spending the day with his father stalking deer no matter how filthy the weather. In fact, the harder the day out, the more William enjoyed himself, proving to his father that he was tough enough and strong enough to keep up with the rest of the party. And, furthermore, he began to prefer hunting, shooting, riding and fishing to the pleasures he enjoyed with his mother in London.

And he didn't mind the fact that with Charles he was expected to dress in a jacket, trousers and brogue shoes, although he wasn't so keen on the strictures placed on him at mealtimes with his grandparents. Then, he would have to arrive at exactly the correct time for meals and behave with the utmost politeness, waiting to be spoken to before being permitted to make any remark. It was all so very different from the fun, slapdash and chaotic mealtimes at home with his mother and younger brother.

Some time after his thirteenth birthday, in June 1995, William discovered girls! As a young child he had always been somewhat precocious and, like many young boys, intrigued by girls of his own age, particularly because he had no sisters. But from the start of his teenage years, William suddenly developed a great interest and fascination in the opposite sex. During beach holidays with his mother, William would always be fascinated with teenage girls, watching them lying in the sun or frolicking in the sea. On one occasion, his mother teased the 14-year-old William for spending most of one morning lying on a beach looking at girls sunbathing topless. And when they wandered down to the sea to swim, still topless, William would immediately sit up and watch their every movement until they returned from their swim and lay down once more.

Occasionally, William would spend hours sitting on the terrace of their holiday villa searching for girls through powerful binoculars. When Diana remonstrated with him, William would reply, 'There's no harm in just looking, you know.' And, with a smile, Diana would walk away in the realisation that her first-born was growing up.

William's interests lay in girls a few years older than himself. When he was 13 and 14 he found himself attracted to girls aged 18 and over, rather than girls of his own age. But at that stage he was just happy to look and see and ask questions. But in October 1995, aged a little over 13, William surprised his mother by asking if he could attend the 'Toff's Ball' at

London's Hammersmith Palais, an annual event for young teenagers of the rich and famous attended by up to 1,000 youngsters.

Such bashes for public school boys and girls have been around since the 1960s. Alcohol, of course, is banned and there are adult chaperones who roam the dance floor checking on the behaviour of all the teenagers, many of whom take the opportunity to go wild. Many do, of course, consume alcohol, taking bottles of vodka and gin from their homes or buying cans of beer from supermarkets and off licences which they purchase after being dropped off by their parents.

The girls and the boys nearly always attend the ball in small groups and spend much of the evening with each other, chatting and dancing together, getting drunk, sharing jokes and generally having tremendous fun. For most it is the first ball they will have attended and getting drunk is one of the favoured intentions. They all know that drinking alcohol will give them Dutch courage and sweep away their teenage inhibitions. They usually consume the drinks in groups outside the venue, throwing back neat vodka, the favourite tipple, and chasing that with cans of strong beer. As a result, of course, many arrive at the ball under the influence of alcohol, if not actually drunk and disorderly. Many of the teenage girls also join in the drinking bouts. Once inside, the girls tend to gather in groups, laughing and giggling and discussing the boys. The teenage lads generally also stay in groups laughing and drinking. As the evening progresses, however, the boys and girls do eventually make contact and dance and chat together.

Given the amount of alcohol consumed and the high spirits of expectant teenagers, the evening is, of course, a recipe for teenage mayhem. That particular ball is often the first time girls and boys of wealthy, well-to-do parents are thrown together on their own with no parental presence. And many do go wild. After similar events in the past, there have been photographs of near-naked revellers, some kissing and smooching and a few even having sex. There are also a number of inebriated, unconscious teenagers.

Prince Charles was against William attending the ball but, with the support of his mother, William persuaded his father to let him attend with a group of his pals from Eton. The result was a near disaster, although William apparently behaved impeccably. At one stage, though, he was followed around the dance hall by a conga line of mini-skirted teenage girls.

'Give me a kiss,' 'Let's dance,' and 'Give me a snog,' were just three of the requests repeated a hundred times to William that night. Some predatory, pushy, wannabe Lolitas were even more aggressive, prepared to take on the four Eton pals who acted as his unofficial bodyguards. The girls wanted to get William to dance, kiss and snog with them with no holds barred. Throughout the ordeal, William smiled and tried to enjoy himself but it was all but impossible for him to relax. Despite the incessant interruptions, William did dance with a number of girls, those who had been introduced to him by his Eton friends, but for the greater part, the dances were wild. No one, however, witnessed the heir to the throne smooching or snogging. And he saw the dance through to the bitter end, leaving with his pals at 2.00am. Reports of the ball were reported sensationally in the tabloid press over the next few days.

Charles read the newspaper reports with horror, and challenged Diana over the incident, wanting to know why she had been so keen to permit William to attend such a wild, drunken near-orgy. The fact that William appeared to have survived the ball, having been party to no embarrassing incidents, did not placate his father. Charles was furious because he had not fully understood that his son was to attend, in reality, more a drunken teenage night of excess and debauchery rather than a ball. It was exactly the sort of publicity that Charles, the Queen and Prince Philip did not need and did not want in 1995 when the royals had been going through such a bad patch, mainly over the separation, divorce and respective love lives of both Charles and Diana. Charles made it perfectly plain that William was never permitted to attend such events and, as a result, William did not attend that particular ball again.

Although not permitted to stick photographs of pin-ups, or anything else, on the walls of his 10ft by 7ft room at Eton, the boys were allowed to put such pictures inside the door of their lockers. Inside William's locker were sexy photos of *Baywatch*'s babe Pamela Lee and Cindy Crawford. Other stars to have graced his locker included Claudia Schiffer and Emma 'Baby Spice' Bunting. He often flicked through magazines checking any of the stars and models he found attractive and, like all boys at Eton, would supplement and change pictures from time to time.

From the age of 13, he would also flick through his mother's magazines, which included both *Vogue* and *Cosmopolitan*. He would scan *Vogue* for great-looking models who appealed to him; but he looked through *Cosmopolitan* reading the articles and educating himself in the facts of life. He was known to fancy the Playboy models, twins Shane and Sia Barbi, who are the living image of the sexy Barbie dolls.

On one occasion, giggling and nudging a

school pal, William summoned his bodyguard to check out a picture of a sexy-looking model in a girlie magazine. Diana saw the three looking admiringly at the magazine and walked over to see what they thought was so interesting. When she realised they were looking at a double-page spread of a girl, she took the magazine, ripped out the page and tore it in two, handing one page to William and the other to the bodyguard.

'What did you do that for?' asked William, somewhat taken aback at his mother's reaction.

'Now you can both share her,' Diana replied and walked away with a smile on her face.

Deadpan, William replied, 'It was only the top halves we wanted.'

William seemed to be gaining a very healthy interest in the opposite sex from about the age of 14, taking every possible opportunity to chat to girls rather than simply ogle magazine photographs. And, unlike many teenage boys, he never seemed to be bashful or shy in their presence.

During winter skiing at Klosters in 1996, William began chatting to an attractive teenage girl while on the slopes and seemed smitten. They chatted and laughed together. For a while they skied together and William suggested they return on the ski-lift together for another downhill run. He then invited her for a bite of lunch, too. But the girl was leaving the following day and they never saw each other again. At the time, William was five years her junior! During the same ski trip, William was much taken by another teenager — the stunning 18-year-old Zoe Cody-Simpson, daughter of an army General. Zoe, who had a marked resemblance to Diana, was invited to join the royal skiing party and spend lunch with them. For two days, Zoe and William skied non-stop together and both seemed to have great fun, William smiling and chatting as though to the manor born.

Since then, he has been encouraged during school holidays to take opportunities to see his cousin Zara Phillips, Peter's sister, and Princess Michael of Kent's daughter, the glamorous Lady Gabriella Windsor, both of whom are just one year older than William.

William was growing up fast and this was displayed not only in his new-found interest in girls. On the playing fields of Eton, William was enjoying a new-found reputation as a fearless, and sometimes aggressive, footballer. At the age of 16, football was William's preferred team sport, in which he usually played right back and was selected to play in his year's first XI. Sometimes his fearlessness ended in real pain.

Playing for Eton against Windsor Boys' School, a traditional local derby, William made a particularly courageous attempt to stop an opposing forward as he tried to crash straight through William's tackle. William was struck in the chest and fell to the ground. Usually in such circumstances, William would immediately get to his feet and continue the game. Not this time. As the game continued, William was seen writhing on the ground. William's housemaster, Dr Gailey, and his private detective ran on to the pitch and the game was stopped. They feared William could be seriously injured.

Despite protestations from his detective,

William played on, though it was obvious that he had not fully recovered. Later that evening, William was seen by the Eton College doctor who diagnosed severely bruised ribs and suggested he might need an X-ray. His parents were informed and Diana telephoned him that evening, shortly after William heard the news of the appalling Dunblane horror in which a deranged gunman shot 13 schoolchildren. Diana wanted to talk about William's accident; William only wanted to talk about the tragedy of Dunblane.

Diana wanted to see William the following day but William told her that he was fine and that it was far more important for her to fly to Scotland to visit the parents of the murdered children. He wouldn't take 'no' for an answer. In the end, Diana accepted her son's protestations. In fact, the decision was taken out of Diana's hands because it was determined by the Queen, advised by palace courtiers, that Charles should fly to Scotland. They realised that if both Charles and Diana flew to Scotland, the media attention would be focused on them being seen together rather than on the grieving parents and the dead children.

A few months later, in July 1996, Prince William, looking older than his 14 years, made the front cover of *Time* magazine. CAN THIS BOY SAVE THE MONARCHY? was the question posed by *Time*. The magazine wrote, 'If the Waleses have damaged the monarchy terribly, they may also have provided its salvation in William, the bright, likeable Prince, beginning to capture the public's imagination. As the divorce brings one act of the royal drama to an end, another one begins, with a fresh and appealing star.'

In November 1996, William was spending his half-term at Balmoral with his father when he shocked animal-lovers around the world by shooting his first stag. Apparently, William was thrilled, for he had brought down the stag with a single shot. And, when William, Charles and other members of the shooting party inspected the dead beast, William was 'blooded' — smeared on the forehead with the blood of the dead animal — just as his father had been when he shot his first stag at

Balmoral 30 years before. William, who has developed into a crack shot, felled the stag with a high-velocity hunting rifle from nearly 150 yards.

The shooting of the stag caused dismay among animal welfare groups while hunters praised his sporting ability. Despite statements saying that William was only involved in a culling exercise, the animal welfare campaigners condemned the shoot outright and castigated Prince Charles for permitting his son to go through with the ritual of killing wild animals. Despite the protests, however, the stag's head has now become a prized trophy, prominently displayed in one of the long rooms at Balmoral. As his prowess with the gun increased, William, often accompanied by Harry and Tiggy, would go for long walks around Balmoral and Sandringham looking for rabbits to shoot. Usually accompanied by a qualified gamekeeper, the three often returned with ten or twelve rabbits in the bag.

Throughout his young life, William has never been afraid to take the initiative, sometimes displaying remarkably adult reactions to events. William did, for example, phone the fashionable San Lorenzo's restaurant to book a table for his unhappy mother and himself in an effort to cheer her up when he was only seven. He happily phoned cinemas to book seats at the age of nine. He also showed powers of leadership when playing football at Ludgrove, encouraging other players and directing team members.

It didn't, therefore, totally surprise his parents when, in 1997, William asked them not to attend the most important day in Eton's year — 4 June — Parents' Day, because he felt the attendance of press and bodyguards might spoil the day for others. They were both even more taken aback when William, totally off his own bat, invited Tiggy to attend instead. Bemused, and not sure how to react, Tiggy phoned her boss, Prince Charles, and asked what she should do. Charles told her to pack a picnic and some chilled bottles of white wine, and go. Tiggy took along one of William's great friends, 16-year-old William van Cutsem, and together they sat on a plaid rug on Agar's Plough — one of the Eton playing fields —

along with hundreds of other boys. That day they ate pâté, sandwiches, crisps and fruit and drank wine.

After lunch, several of William's friends came over to sit and chat and have a glass of wine and, at one stage, they were joined by three mini–skirted teenage girls who stayed to chat for 15 minutes. William seemed very effusive, laughing and joking while Tiggy looked on, acting like a big sister. After lunch, William and another friend called William went walkabout, moving from party to party, chatting to Eton pals and their parents and being introduced to scores of pretty girls, sisters and friends of friends. Dressed in his Eton uniform coat and tails, William was in great form, smiling, shaking hands and chatting to the girls he met. The teenage boy was rapidly becoming a young man.

11

Death of a Princess

Prince William was holidaying at Balmoral in
Scotland with his brother Harry, his father
Prince Charles, and the Queen and Prince
Philip, when he heard of the tragedy that
shattered his young life. The appalling crash
which killed his beloved mother occurred in
the tunnel beneath the Pont de l'Alma beside
the River Seine in Paris occurred 30 minutes
after midnight (11.30pm British Summer
Time) on Sunday, 31 August 1997.

At the exact time, William and Harry

were sleeping peacefully. They had spoken to their mother only a few hours earlier when she had phoned from Paris and had gone to bed before 10.00pm that night. The initial report of the incident, stating that Diana had been involved in a fatal car accident, was passed through the usual government channels, according to the designated protocol. The duty officer of the French Interior Ministry telephoned his counterpart at the British Embassy in Paris some time after 1.00am French time. In turn, he immediately called the duty officer at the British Ambassador's residence in Paris who woke the Ambassador, Sir Michael Jay, informing him of the accident.

At that stage, it was understood that Diana had only been injured and that none of her injuries were life-threatening, but French police had confirmed the deaths of both her lover, Dodi Fayed, and the driver of the Mercedes, Henri Paul. The news of the accident was flashed from the British Embassy in Paris to the Foreign Office duty officer in London, who, in turn, called Buckingham Palace, giving the few details then known of the accident. However, when French doctors reported that there serious concerns over the extent of Diana's injuries, the decision was taken to telephone Balmoral and suggest that Prince Charles should be wakened and informed of everything that was then known. The duty police officer at Balmoral, who also doubled as duty night telephonist, took the call and phoned Charles's valet.

Shortly after 2.00am BST, the duty valet knocked on Charles's bedroom door and told him what had happened. Charles immediately phoned Buckingham Palace and asked to be kept informed, directly, of any developments. He phoned Sir Robert Fellowes, the Queen's Principal Private Secretary, Diana's brother-in-law, who happened to be staying at Balmoral that weekend and, together, they decided only to wake and inform the Queen if Diana's condition deteriorated further.

One hour later, the news came through that Diana had died. It was 3.00am BST and Charles was wide awake, sitting by the phone, waiting for further news of Diana's condition which he knew would come at some stage that night. But even he was not prepared for the news of her death. He was shocked, stunned that something like that could have occurred to Diana who was always so careful when driving in cars, always wearing her seat belt, never taking risks on the road and never driving too fast.

After thanking the duty officer at Buckingham Palace, Charles sat still for a few seconds taking in the unbelievable news and deciding precisely what he should do. He decided to let William and Harry sleep on through the night rather than wake them with such distressing and shocking news. He knew he must inform his mother immediately, and called her telling her of the appalling tragedy. She asked Charles to dress and come immediately to her room. Charles dressed quickly and went to his mother's bedroom, telling her the scant details he knew. After Charles had told his mother everything, the Queen phoned Prince Philip, telling him of the tragedy and inviting him to come and hear what Charles had to say.

What concerned all three was how and

when the news should be broken to William and Harry. There was grave concern how Harry, only 12, would cope with the terrible tragedy and so, together, the decision was taken to let the boys, who slept in adjoining bedrooms, sleep on. Charles said that he would wait until the boys were wide awake before giving them the devastating news of their mother's death. By then he hoped to have far more details of exactly what had happened so that he could answer any questions the boys might ask.

Charles shaved, showered and dressed before 7.00am so he would be prepared and ready for the terrible ordeal of telling his sons what had happened to their mother. After the two young princes had been awake for 15 minutes or so, Charles went to see them in their rooms. He told them all he knew of the accident but he did tell them directly that their mother had died, along with her friend Dodi Fayed. No further details of that conversation are known but, immediately afterwards, Charles took the boys to see the Queen and Prince Philip who also were dressed, ready for the day. For 20 minutes William and Harry, with Charles, the Queen and Prince Philip, discussed the matter and they comforted the boys but no details are known of that meeting.

Charles telephoned Tiggy Legge-Bourke, the one young woman Charles knew could be depended upon to handle such a crisis. He knew that both William and Harry, who had known Tiggy for five years, put great trust in her and were very fond of her. When Charles phoned Tiggy, shortly after breakfast on that fateful Sunday, and told her of the dreadful news, she immediately offered to fly to Scotland to be of whatever help and comfort she could to William and Harry. Charles was greatly relieved because he knew that of all the people the boys knew well, Tiggy was closest of all, closer than any of their aunts or any other members of the Royal Family. Charles also realised that the boys would be totally natural with Tiggy, and not try to act courageously, bottling up their feelings of sadness, loss and distress. He knew from experience that the boys had to live with the fact that from that moment on they had no mother, and Charles believed that the warm-hearted Tiggy would be the one person able to talk to them and encourage them to release their emotions in their time of grief. Charles was well aware that both William and Harry knew, and had known for some years, that Tiggy cared deeply for them.

When they had showered and dressed, Charles encouraged the boys to accompany him to breakfast because he did not want them to stay alone in their rooms with the pain of the tragedy. He knew they should meet their grandparents and eat something, and breakfast was the one informal meal of the day at Balmoral. All the family and guests are allowed to arrive in the dining room at whatever time they wish, help themselves to whatever they want from a table at the side of the room, while footmen serve tea or coffee.

On that fateful Sunday, the Queen and Prince Philip made the effort to come down to breakfast early, joining Charles, William and Harry, so they would feel they were in the bosom of their family. After breakfast, Charles asked his sons whether they wanted to go church that Sunday morning and stressed that if they didn't want to attend, if they didn't feel strong enough, then everyone would understand. Harry looked at William, who looked at his father, and asked if he was planning on attending the morning service. It was, of course, a tradition of the Royal Family that whenever they stay at Balmoral the entire family attends Crathie church, the small, local church near Balmoral, every Sunday. Charles said that he intended to accompany the Queen and Prince Philip and William said that he, too, would like to go. Harry promptly said that he would also join his father and his brother.

So, after breakfast, they all went back upstairs to change. Dressed in grey suits and black ties, William and Harry sat either side of their father for the short car drive to and from the church. Their faces were almost expressionless and the parishioners, television cameramen, photographers and journalists who gathered to see the family were amazed to see not a tear shed by either William or young Harry. The composure of both boys was remarkable, revealing how, in a matter of just three hours, they had managed to compose themselves and then, somehow, cope with the pressure of appearing in public without breaking down or shedding a single tear.

But throughout that awful Sunday and the days that followed, both William and Harry would break down in tears many times. During that first week, William and, more frequently, Harry would sometimes burst into tears spontaneously, suddenly remembering that they would never again see their mother. On those occasions, both Charles and Tiggy would comfort and console them, sometimes just putting an arm around them as they walked in the grounds of Balmoral, not needing to say a word, but just handing them a handkerchief to wipe their eyes, giving them time to collect their emotions once more.

The scenes at Balmoral during the days following Diana's death were, understandably, traumatic for everyone, but particularly for William and Harry. The Queen and Prince Philip tried, in their own way, to comfort the boys but there had never been a close, loving relationship between the boys and their paternal grandparents. The Queen's strong, unemotional character had been forged in an earlier generation and, even her own children would confess in their maturity that their mother had generally been reserved and cold in moments of crisis. They all respected her for the work and the commitment she showed to the nation. And Prince Philip had been even more distant, for the most part treating his three sons as junior midshipmen rather than young boys needing help, advice and paternal love.

Charles understood this only too well and he didn't want to leave his sons alone at this distressing time and yet he knew it was his duty to fly to France to recover Diana's body, leaving William and Harry at Balmoral. Before his departure, he discussed the matter with his sons, explaining why he had to go. It was his duty to bring back the body of their mother and he could not shirk from doing so. They understood that and urged their father to go. Before he left, however, he promised to return to Balmoral to be with them that same night. William told his father that he understood, that he thought it right and proper that Charles should go to Paris. Indeed, William volunteered to accompany his father to France and return with his mother's body, but Charles asked him instead to stay behind to care for Harry until Tiggy arrived. William agreed.

Charles told his sons that if Diana's brother Charles Spencer had been living in England, then it would have been perfectly right and proper for him to fly to Paris and accompany the body back home, along with Diana's sisters. But as he was then living in South Africa, there was no way he could reach Paris in so short a time. Both William and Harry understood the predicament and they both told their father they were happy that he wanted to carry out the task. Both lads felt that their father had jumped at the opportunity to be close to their mother, the woman he had married and then divorced, the woman he had left by walking out of the marriage and moving to Highgrove. Now, it seemed to William, that in death his parents were to be far closer than during their life and that one, single, deliberate act brought William closer to his father.

Charles's decision to take charge of everything, to care for Diana in her death, had a remarkable impact on William's relationship with his father. From that decision grew a bond between Charles and William which has become stronger than anything between them during the years of Diana's life. In those days leading up to Diana's funeral and beyond, young William's relationship with his father changed dramatically and he felt closer to his father, more respectful, and he felt that his father actually loved him, whereas before William had sometimes wondered how loving his father really was towards him. Now he knew and the thought comforted him.

During that first day at Balmoral, especially when Charles had to leave for Paris, young Harry became emotionally distraught and, before Tiggy arrived to comfort and look after him, William assumed the role of big brother. During that Sunday, Harry was inseparable from his brother and William seemed to mature almost by the hour. William decided everything that day, taking all the decisions which Harry was happy to follow.

And that was a dramatic change of character for Harry who is known as a most independent young man, usually far more independent of spirit than William. Diana used to say that before reaching a decision she could always discuss matters with William, but Harry preferred to take instant decisions without consultation, wanting to do whatever he pleased, rather than worrying about what everyone else wanted to do.

William decided that they should play games inside, go for walks together in the autumn sunshine and kick a football around. In fact, they only kicked a football around for a few seconds. They both sensed that it was all wrong for them to be playing football only hours after their mother had died and so, almost immediately, they stopped playing and continued instead to walk together around the castle grounds.

William realised that he had to keep Harry's mind occupied, to stop him thinking of their mother and her appalling death. As one longstanding member of the Royal Household commented, 'Overnight, William became a young man. He even seemed to grow in stature, taking command of Harry in a remarkably warm fashion, walking around the estate with his arm around his shoulders, talking to him whenever the tears flowed, comforting him, urging him to think only of the wonderful times they had together with their mother.' But Harry could not be comforted and throughout the first couple of days he would simply ask, over and over again, 'Why? Why? Why did she die?'

At night, William would ensure that Harry was asleep before he went to bed, even though both his father and Tiggy were at Balmoral to care for Harry. But after the arrival of Tiggy, William became more introvert, despite the strong relationship he had always enjoyed with Tiggy whom he had always treated as an older sister. Harry needed Tiggy's warmth, her open arms, her gentleness and her understanding. For much of that first week, Harry spent the days walking around Balmoral with Tiggy and in the evening he would sit with her, cuddling up to her, needing her emotional stability and quiet strength. And

Tiggy would sit with her arm around Harry, almost cradling him. She gave him the comfort he needed to face the reality which scared him. And William spent those days close to his father, chatting together as they had hardly done before, going for long walks around Balmoral, simply spending time together.

Some time later, William would say how those days with his father had given him the emotional strength he needed, enabling him to come to terms with the death of his beloved mother. William also realised, as he never had before, that he now needed his father more than anyone else in the world. Charles would just let William chat away about anything, letting all his emotions run their natural course. Twice they went fly-fishing together, a sport William enjoys in the same way as his father, affording days alone by a fast-flowing river, away from the cares of the world, alone with his thoughts.

Prince Charles wanted to involve both William and Harry in drawing up the details of their mother's funeral. Their uncle Charles Spencer, along with their aunts, Jane Fellowes and Sarah McCorquodale, had said they also wanted to be involved in planning their sister's funeral because they felt Diana would not have wanted a staid, royal affair full of protocol and historic precedence. Prince Charles discussed this with William and Harry and they both agreed that, if possible, their mother's funeral should reflect her life, the people she respected, the charities she helped, rather than a church full of dignitaries, titled families, ambassadors and politicians whom she had hardly ever met and, in her lifetime, didn't want to know. And Charles Spencer, Jane and Sarah also wanted a special, extraordinary funeral service, a funeral that Diana herself would have wanted, representing her life and her interests rather than those of the Royal Family, the Establishment or the State. And they wanted William and Harry to offer their views as to the sort of funeral their mother would have wanted. Both boys welcomed that.

Throughout that first week, both William and Harry seemed riveted to the television screen, wanting to learn all they could of the details surrounding the death of their mother.

Together, they would watch as many news items as they could hoping to learn something new, something that might throw light on how and why their mother had died. William quickly became convinced that it was the paparazzi who were responsible for the accident and, therefore, in his mind, responsible for her death. And William went further. He considered that if the paparazzi were indeed responsible for his mother's death then, in fact, they had all but murdered her.

Over the years, William had come to hate the paparazzi, indeed, any photographers or cameramen who dogged Diana every time she ventured out of Kensington Palace. William had seen his mother break down in tears when chased by the photographers; he had seen the effect chasing cameramen had on her when she would arrive home, her make-up smudged, the tears drying on her cheeks, her emotions almost at breaking point due entirely to the intrusive behaviour of the paparazzi. Since the age of 12, William had come to hate the paparazzi with a passion and both Charles and Diana needed, from time to time, to tell him that the press, the newspapers, the television stations and the paparazzi were the link between the monarchy and the people, the messengers whose job it was to inform the nation of royal matters. For the most part, William understood this but he could never forgive and would never forget the behaviour of the rat pack that chased, dogged and humiliated his mother at every conceivable opportunity.

But William became convinced that the paparazzi were completely responsible for his mother's death. He believed that if the photographers had not been chasing his mother that night there would have been no need for the chauffeur, Henri Paul, to race at speeds in excess of 100mph through the streets of Paris and, therefore, there would have been no crash. And his mother would still be alive. Ever since the accident, no one has been able to persuade William otherwise. There is in William the same stubborn streak that was part of Diana's character and, no matter what people might persuade him to say or do or accept, young William will come to his own conclusions and keep to them.

Throughout her life, Diana showed she could be wonderfully stubborn, especially when senior Buckingham Palace courtiers would try to advise her, telling her how to behave or what to do. Diana would listen to what they had to say, often nodding in agreement — and then she would go and do exactly what she wanted, taking no notice whatsoever of the advice the courtiers had given her. Indeed, Diana would sometimes behave in exactly the same way with Charles, especially when their marriage was falling apart in the 1980s. Diana would come to an arrangement, or an agreement, with Charles and then happily go and do whatever she wished without even informing Charles that she had no intention of carrying out the agreement they had reached. And that, Diana knew, infuriated Charles.

But also during that painful week, William watched the television news bulletins and special programmes with astonishment as the nation poured out its heart for his mother. Of course, William had some idea that his mother was the star of the Royal Family; he knew that whenever she appeared in public, women, in particular, would turn out to cheer her, even in the cold and the pouring rain. William knew that his mother had built up a special relationship with the British people and, on the few occasions he accompanied his mother on official or unofficial engagements, he would see for himself the reaction of the people to his mother's appearance. He sensed that the ordinary women of Britain really loved his mother in a way that they had never loved any other members of the Royal Family. There was an affinity, an understanding, a special relationship between his mother and tens of thousands of women she had never met and never talked to. Watching the scenes of genuine sorrow as tens of thousands of people milled around Kensington Palace and Buckingham Palace day and night would reduce William to tears, so moved was he that so many ordinary people felt such genuine affection for his mother.

To William, there seemed an almost magical relationship which he could not quite understand. He had seen the general public react to his father but there had never been such a spontaneous outpouring of emotion, almost of love and affection, as the public showed towards his mother. Now, as he sat in front of the television at Balmoral, William realised just how close his mother had come to the British people, revealing an extraordinarily, deep relationship. It did not seem to matter that the hundreds of thousands who flocked to London to pay their respects to his mother had never met her for most had never even seen her in the flesh. But that didn't seem to matter, Diana had overcome that hurdle. As the television replayed footage of her life, William came to understand for the first time the relationship that had developed between his mother and the British people.

The same people who now flooded into London with their bunches of flowers, their messages of grief and their tears were the same people who had also wept tears at his mother's magnificent wedding in 1981. The same people had watched his mother's progress, enraptured by her smile and her kind, caring nature. They had felt happy for her when she gave birth to William and then, two years later, to Harry. They had watched the sparkle go out of Diana's eyes, watched her grow thin, painfully thin, and they understood that something was not right in her marriage. They saw the signs and they understood and worried for her as if she was one of their daughters or a close friend. There was nothing they could do but show their support for her whenever she appeared in public. But when news leaked out that Charles had returned to his former mistress, Camilla Parker Bowles, the sympathy for his mother turned to anger towards Charles for many of those cheering, sympathetic women had also been married to cheating, lying husbands and they understood the pain that Diana was going through.

During the week following his mother's death, William spent hours sitting in front of the television watching the tearful crowds, the history of his mother's short life and hearing 'experts' dissect the breakdown of her marriage. William would say later that he learned more about his mother during that week than he had ever known before.

It must have been distressing enough for the young princes to come to terms with the fact of Diana's death, and also to have to endure the constant examination and re-examination of her life through every aspect of the media — and occasionally, they would feel surprised and even shocked at how little they knew of certain aspects of her life.

As though in a trance, William watched the television footage of his mother's remarkable progress from the shy teenager who dated Prince Charles to her wonderful wedding day, from being the mother to the heirs to the throne to the tragedy of being spurned by the man she had loved. It showed Diana change from being a kindergarten nurse to becoming an outstanding international icon of the late twentieth century. The film clips also showed her battling with the agonies of anorexia and loneliness, and also the extraordinary strength of character which enabled her to devote her life to others less privileged. It also made William proud that he was his mother's son.

It was during this harrowing week that William learned for the first time the extent to which his mother had been loved by the entire nation. He came to understand how his mother had won over the great mass of the British people, and many others across the world. He witnessed in that footage a part of her life that he had never really seen before because most of the overseas work she had carried out during term time when William was at school, to a great extent unaware of the magnificent work she was carrying out for charitable causes.

Those films revealed to William that it had been his mother's tireless charity work, dedicating her life to the disadvantaged, the homeless and the underprivileged, to lepers and orphans, to cancer patients, AIDS victims and those maimed by landmines, that had won her the respect of everyone. And she had achieved this by the manner of her involvement, giving of herself to those she visited, showing them love, holding and touching them, talking to them, showing her warmth and her concern. She had touched a chord in the nation and had won not only their respect but also their admiration and, more importantly, their love.

William was also affected by the thousands of children who came with their parents to lay flowers, leave cards and, sometimes, their favourite teddy bears and dolls for his mother, wanting to give something of themselves to a woman they understood had the power to reduce their own mothers to tears at the moment of her death. William was affected by the thousands of people who happily waited for hours simply to sign a book of condolence for his mother; who brought armfuls of flowers — or sometimes just a single flower — to show their love and reveal their grief; a river of people standing in stunned silence with but one simple mission, to show their love.

Almost spellbound, William could not leave the television screen, taken aback by the overwhelming scenes he was witnessing. He was amazed at the open displays of grief, the quiet sobbing of so many people, who revealed their suffering and their sorrow in scenes which London had never before witnessed. The stiff upper lip which he knew his father and grandfather, as well as his friends at Eton, still believed in, and which William understood to be a part of the British character had gone, to be replaced by open displays of grief.

Most of the time, William sat alone in front of the television that week, taking in everything the news bulletins reported and examined in the greatest detail. Occasionally, Tiggy and sometimes Harry would join him, but they were not so keenly interested in dissecting each and every piece of evidence that was debated by the journalists and so-called experts. William could not be dissuaded from his firm belief that the principal reason the crash occurred was due entirely to the chasing pack of photographers. He understood that the chauffeur should not have been driving when under the influence of drink or at such excessive speeds, and he understood that his beloved mother should have been wearing her seat belt.

William found it unbelievable that his mother wasn't wearing a seat belt that night for she had always been strict about the practice whenever she was a passenger in a car. Indeed, she would never even permit a car to move off unless she had checked that William and Harry, and anyone else in the vehicle, were correctly belted into their seats. Always, always, Diana herself would check their belts or she would ask the police officer travelling with them to do so. William found it difficult to believe that his mother would set off from the Ritz Hotel without her seat belt fastened. And William simply could not believe that his mother would not have secured her belt when she realised the excessive speeds they were travelling that night.

William would talk to Tiggy about all these matters which were not debated to any great degree on the television, and William wondered why such vitally important aspects were glossed over. Sometimes, William wanted to grab a phone and call the television stations to tell them that his mother would never have driven at such high speeds in any car if she had not been wearing a seat belt. To William, it just didn't make sense. And he was perplexed.

William would stay up late during that first week wanting to capture every moment of the TV coverage as the cameras captured the mood of the nation. He wanted to go to London to mingle with the people who had showed so much love for his mother. On her behalf, William wanted to thank them personally, each and everyone of them who had made the journey to London with their flowers, their cards, their messages and their gifts for his mother. William knew that his mother would have been amazed at the outpouring of tears and affection for her at the time of her death and he wanted to be a part of it.

He wanted to join the all-night vigils in the royal parks; he wanted to queue with the ordinary people who sometimes waited for eight hours or more simply to write a few words in one of the 30 books of condolence that were needed to cope with the extraordinary demand. William wanted to be a part of the people's grief, sharing at first hand their sorrow and their torment. He understood that, like him, many who came to London were suffering symptoms of the sort of intense personal grief that people usually only experience after the sudden and unexpected loss of somebody close to them. Many of those who felt compelled to flock to London to show their love knew so much about Diana that many had come to believe that they knew her extremely well. The fact that Diana was so young, so beautiful, and so vulnerable and a mother heightened the grief.

William urged Charles and later the Queen to let him go to London to thank everyone personally for the gifts of flowers they had brought to show their love for Diana. But the Queen refused the request saying that such an act would not be appropriate for a young prince, barely 15 years old. In fact, those courtiers who advise the Queen, advised that William should not be permitted to go to London and mingle with the mourners because of the upsurge of emotion that might cause amongst the tens of thousands who had come to London to share in the sense of loss.

There was also another point. In the last years of her life, Diana had so completely outshone the rest of the Royal Family, much to the chagrin of the Queen, Prince Philip and her advisers, that Diana had earned far more respect and love from the nation than the monarch herself. William did not, therefore, get the opportunity to meet the people, but his instinct, to go and see the thousands of mourners, and thank them for their flowers and their cards, had been the right one. And that instinct, displayed by William was precisely the action his mother would have taken in similar circumstances. Like mother, like son. But it was not to be. In the same way that Buckingham Palace advisers through the years had prevented Diana carrying out such mould-breaking ideas, now the powers-that-be had stopped William in his bid to say a public 'thank you' for those who were showing their love for his mother.

William pleaded with his father to let him go to London, but Charles could not do such a thing and, thereby, contradict the decision his mother had made. Charles tried to placate William, telling him that it was the Queen who made those decisions. The Queen, as monarch, was the head of the entire Royal

Family and, as such, she would be the one to lead the family mourners. William was frustrated and angry but he knew there was nothing he could do.

By the middle of the week, however, there were growing rumbles of discontent among the mourners which were loudly and brazenly trumpeted by the tabloid press complaining that the Royal Family, and the Queen in particular, had not shown sufficient public grief over Diana's death. Despite statements from Buckingham Palace and Downing Street, however, recording the Queen's and the family's grief, the public would not be placated. Buckingham Palace announced that the Royal Family were mourning in private, supporting William and Harry in their hour of need, but many mourners were not sure that this was true. They believed that many of those who were close to the Queen were not unhappy that Diana, Princess of Wales, who had eclipsed the entire Royal Family, had left the scene for ever. The British public knew that, to many advisers, Diana had become such a powerful person in her own right, a person whom the nation had taken to its heart to such a degree that the Royal Family had been all but overlooked as of little or no importance.

Despite the Queen's adamant refusal to permit William to travel to London and mingle with the people, William continued to press his father to be permitted to go, to demonstrate that he wanted to thank them personally for sharing his grief at the death of his mother.

'I should be there, I should be there,' he said time and again. 'And I know Mother would want me to do this, to say thank you to everyone.'

William, of course, was right. Diana would have applauded her son for behaving in such a way, making his own decision to go and thank everyone for their kindness, understanding and love. But William was prevented, unable to follow his instincts. The men of power who advised the Queen had moved in to re-impose the authority of the monarch after years of seeing that power slowly eroded by Diana.

As William sat watching television, he

actually leapt into the air and cheered when he heard his uncle, Earl Charles Spencer, make a statement to the world before flying to London from his home in South Africa.

'All those who have come into contact with Diana,' Earl Spencer said, 'particularly over the last 17 years, will share my family's grief. She was unique. She understood the most precious needs of human beings, particularly those who suffered. Her vibrancy, combined with a very real sense of duty, has now gone for ever. It is heartbreaking to lose such a human being, especially as she was only 36. This is not a time for recriminations, but for sadness. However, I would say that I always believed the press would kill her in the end. But not even I could imagine that they would take such a direct hand in her death as seems to be the case. It would appear that every proprietor and editor of every publication that has paid for intrusive, exploitative photographs of her, encouraging greedy and ruthless individuals to risk everything in pursuit of Diana's image, has blood on their hands today.'

When those words were repeated on

later news bulletins, William sat with tears of anger and frustration in his eyes. He agreed with every single word his uncle had said. Like him, there was now someone else in the family who believed that the press were responsible for his mother's death. And William believed there were millions more across the country who shared that belief.

Both William and Harry waited up to see their father when he returned to Balmoral after escorting Diana's body back to Britain. They had watched the live television pictures of the Queen's Flight landing at RAF Northolt in West London bringing the body of their mother back home. They watched, mostly in silence, as their mother's body was taken from the aircraft, the coffin draped in a Royal Standard and a ten-man bearer party from the Queen's Colour Squadron of the RAF Regiment escorting the coffin to the waiting hearse. No one can know what thoughts passed through their minds at that moment, for this was the first time that they had seen real evidence that their mother was indeed dead.

Tiggy sat with them watching, replying to

Harry's questions which, for the most part, she was able to answer though she was no expert on protocol and procedure for such occasions. After the hearse had driven away under police escort, the boys saw their father climb aboard the aircraft for his return flight to Scotland. Three hours later, he arrived back at Balmoral and William and Harry greeted him as though they had not seen him for weeks. That night, more than any other night, William and Harry needed their father to be close to them. Shortly after 10.00pm, William and Harry went to bed; it had been the longest day in their young lives.

When their uncle Earl Spencer arrived at Balmoral two days later, on Tuesday, 2 September along with their aunts, Lady Jane Fellowes and Sarah McCorquodale, the Queen had already decided that she would like the Spencer family to be intimately involved in planning Diana's funeral. It is customary in royal circles that funerals of members of the Royal Family are enshrined in strict protocol, something which Diana fought against all her life. So the Queen suggested that Prince

Charles and Earl Spencer, together with Diana's sisters, Jane and Sarah, as well as both William and Harry, should form a committee to plan and oversee the funeral details as well as the church service. Sir Robert Fellowes, the Queen's Principal Private Secretary — William and Harry's uncle by marriage — would also sit on the committee to offer advice and represent the Queen's views.

The committee, with William and Harry in attendance, met on the Tuesday and Wednesday of that week. Sometimes, they asked advice from other people and Sir Robert Fellowes was in constant contact with Prime Minister Tony Blair's senior officials at Downing Street. Tony Blair offered to help in any way he could and asked to be kept informed of the plans for the funeral service. Police chiefs in London were also kept informed and asked for their advice on the route the funeral cortège should take and the necessary safety measures that should be implemented to safeguard the million or more people expected to flock to London to pay their last respects to the princess they adored.

William and Harry were both invited to participate in the planning and, before any decision was taken, William, in particular, was asked for his views, and invited to consider how his mother might have approved of the plans being put forward.

For the most part, Harry would look for guidance from both William and his father. William usually supported the view put forward by his uncle because he believed that Earl Spencer felt the same way as he did. The statement that Earl Spencer made before leaving South Africa had made a deep and favourable impression on William and, as a result, he came to trust the opinion of his mother's brother. William became increasingly involved in the planning, putting forward ideas and commenting enthusiastically whenever it was suggested that protocol would not be observed.

William was especially happy when the suggestion was made that representatives from Diana's favourite charities should be invited to attend the funeral service in Westminster Abbey in place of the usual list of statesmen, politicians, ambassadors and representatives from other countries. And he liked the fact that Diana's friends should be invited and given pride of place in the Abbey. William understood, perhaps more than anyone else, that since her marriage, Diana had been determined to maintain friendships with non-royal friends. And now it seemed that in her death those friends would not be forgotten. And William was thrilled when the decision was taken to invite Elton John to sing a new version of his famous hit 'Candle in The Wind' because William knew his mother loved that simple, moving song.

William was relieved, but not fully satisfied, when, five days after Diana's death, the Queen finally decided that the Royal Family should make a public appearance — but not in London. On Thursday, 4 September, the Queen and Prince Philip drove to the gates of Balmoral Castle and inspected the flowers placed outside by people from nearby villages. William knew in his heart that such a gesture was not sufficient to show the British public that the Royal Family had really cared for

Diana.

Moreover, William was even more frustrated when his grandmother agreed to permit Prince Andrew and his brother Prince Edward to make an 'impromptu' walkabout along the Mall outside Buckingham Palace, chat to the mourners, and sign one of the books of condolence. William had wanted to do just that. He had pleaded to do so days earlier but he had been refused. Now, others, who were not members of his mother's family, were being given permission to carry out a duty which William believed was his prerogative — and his alone.

William argued this with his father, pleading with him to go to the Queen and tell her that William was no longer a child but wanted to shoulder the responsibility that was rightly his as his mother's eldest son. Charles, however, was in a difficult predicament. He had hardly ever argued with his mother over any matter, prepared to accept her word on any subject simply because she was the monarch and he had been brought up almost to revere her. Charles did, however, talk the matter over with the Queen and told her how William desperately wanted to go to London to mix with the crowds and thank them personally for their heart-warming and emotional response to his mother's death.

William's uncle, Charles Spencer, asked the Queen whether he would be allowed to visit London and thank everyone for the warmth of their response to Diana's death. And this, too, was refused. He was not even permitted to join Andrew and Edward, which he believed was totally and manifestly unfair.

As a result, Andrew and Edward were, therefore, the first members of the Royal Family to appear in London before the grieving nation. William watched them on television and he felt deep frustration and anger that he had not been permitted to go to London to thank the people.

William also felt angry when the Queen agreed to make an 'unprecedented' television address to the nation, announcing that Diana's funeral service would be a 'unique funeral for a unique person'. Her short speech may have been a brilliant public relations exercise, but failed to make William feel any less resentful. He accepted that, officially, the stuffy protocol that his mother had fought against all her adult life was to be thrown out and the plans put forward by the 'family committee' had been approved. But, in his young mind, William knew that all the decisions being taken concerning his mother's funeral were pitched in such a way so as to restore the reputation and authority of the Queen. And William felt that the death and the funeral of his darling mother were being hijacked by the royal courtiers and manipulated for their own ends. To William, it seemed his mother's family, the Spencers, were not being given the freedom to handle her death and her funeral as they thought fit.

Charles Spencer was well aware how the Windsors had behaved towards Diana. She had told her brother that she had never wanted to separate from Charles, nor had she ever wanted a divorce. But both separation and divorce had been forced upon her by the Queen, Prince Philip and the royal advisers. Prince Charles's wishes had also been ignored for he had agreed with Diana — there had been no need for them to divorce. Charles was quite happy that he and Diana should have remained married but Prince Philip, in particular, and many advisers were adamant that the divorce should go through, and by doing so, of course, Diana would no longer be an official member of the Royal Family.

And William also knew of his mother's wishes. Diana had confessed to William that she had never wanted an official separation or a divorce from his father. They were living separate lives quite happily with Diana remaining in London at Kensington Palace and Charles living at Highgrove. Whenever Charles needed to stay overnight in London, then he had his own apartment at St James's. Both Diana and Charles believed that William and Harry would be happier if they remained married but lived separate lives in separate homes. Neither Charles nor Diana had wanted to put their sons through the trauma and public humiliation of witnessing a divorce in the full glare of the media. Diana believed that the boys could handle the unofficial separation quite happily, sharing their time between their mother and father. What both boys hated above all else was the private lives of their parents being splashed all over the newspapers week after week.

William would confess later that he hated the publicity that had surrounded his parents' marriage break-up. It not only made him feel sad and lonely but made him feel sorry for them, both of them, having to endure being constantly ridiculed and humiliated by the press simply because their marriage hadn't worked out as it should. And it was difficult for young William to accept that the family which had rejected his mother in life, was now intent on maintaining as much control over her funeral arrangements as possible after her death.

All this was understood by Prince William as it was understood by other members of the Spencer family. And, as a result, when the moment came for William to be permitted to walk behind his mother's coffin, he was determined to do so. He knew that his prescence, and that of his brother and

Charles Spencer, would show to the world the dual links his mother had with the Royal Family and the Spencers.

At one of the committee meetings, William read out a newspaper article which emphasised that strict protocol was reserved for the state funerals of monarchs or top-rank generals, winners of wars and famous prime ministers. But, the article continued, because Diana was none of these she should be awarded a lower-rank funeral. William wanted to know what sort of funeral his mother would receive. It was as a result of that committee meeting that the idea of a 'special funeral' was put forward, which meant that the Royal Family could neatly side-step the potentially controversial issue without causing offence to Diana's memory. But William knew what was happening.

The great mass of the population, however, wanted Diana to have a splendid, magnificent funeral. These were the people who had followed her career from innocent kindergarten teacher to the world's most loved princess, who had cared deeply for her, who had accepted her as royalty's superstar, the people's princess. So they, too, demanded a unique funeral for her. Traditional protocol decreed that the funeral procession was a matter for the palace courtiers; new protocol said that the people's princess should be seen by all those who wanted to pay their respects to her cortège. Old protocol said that the monarch was not required to offer a public tribute to the deceased princess; new protocol said that the Queen should be publicly harangued in the press until she did. Old protocol made no provision for a pop star to sing at such a funeral; new protocol invited Elton John.

What occurred throughout Britain in that extraordinary, memorable week was unprecedented in the history of the monarchy. Protocol and tradition, rejected and resented by Diana, was turned on its head. And one of the people responsible was none other than her own son, William, who was then only 15 years of age. The British nation, however, had no idea that young William had played such a leading role in such a monumental change of practice in royal traditions which, until then, had for centuries been dictated by faceless, grey men whose lives were ruled by protocol. The people, the monarch's subjects who shop in the supermarkets, go to football matches, drink in pubs, play bingo and the National Lottery and are addicted to TV soaps, had made their voices felt and changed the status of protocol. They had no idea that in young William's heart beat the same disdain for tradition as his mother had fought against for so many years. Now he was carrying the banner, taking over where his mother had left off.

William's persistence, however, finally paid off. He had forced the issue and a reluctant Queen had finally caved in and permitted young William and Harry to walk among the mourners outside Kensington Palace, to say 'thank you' to a tiny handful of the million or more who had flocked to say 'goodbye' to Diana. Accompanied by his brother, William looked far older than his 15 years as he chatted to the ordinary men, women and children who had travelled to

London specifically to say their farewells to Diana.

Charles, Tiggy Legge-Bourke, William and Harry flew from Aberdeen to RAF Northolt in West London earlier that day and had gone to the boys' old home, Kensington Palace, where they used to stay with their mother at weekends and during school holidays. That return visit to their mother's home was traumatic for both the boys. William and Harry wondered around the apartment, collecting their personal items, some clothes they had always kept there and books and photographs. School uniforms and other items that they would need for the new school term had already been packed and sent to Highgrove. In the drawing room where Diana spent most of her time, the room was still full of the photographs she had framed, nearly all pictures of William and Harry from their earliest childhood moments to the present day. The photographs covered one wall as well as two tables, all Diana's favourite pictures, showing that Diana did indeed attach great importance to the job of motherhood as well as showing her harshest critics the love she bore her two boys. William also looked into his mother's old suite of rooms but only for a moment for the memories were too stark, too recent for him to keep his nerve. And there was a public engagement to face.

Dressed in suits and wearing black ties, William and Harry, accompanied by their father, walked out unannounced from Kensington Palace, through the gates that had become a shrine to Diana. The crowds bringing flowers, reading the messages of condolence, checking the gifts left on the palace gates, were taken by surprise on seeing Prince Charles, William and Harry walk casually out of the gates. Their appearance mesmerised the waiting crowds as well as the hard-nosed TV cameramen, photographers and journalists who were waiting outside. William, in particular, looked remarkably at ease, the handsome young teenager, tall for his age, an imposing figure, smiling broadly and keen to meet and chat and shake the hands of the throng of people standing behind the barriers. To everyone, William and Harry just kept repeating 'Thank you, thank you,' over and over again.

But they were not only saying 'thank you' for the gifts of flowers pressed into their hands, but on behalf of their mother to whom the visitors had come to pay their respects and show their love. At first, the boys seemed taken aback by the sheer volume of floral tributes in front of the black and gold iron gates, but they relaxed as soon as they began talking to those who wanted to shake their hands and give them flowers. Over and over, as William and Harry spoke or listened to the well-wishers, the princes offered their gratitude for the shared sense of loss. They grasped as many out-stretched hands as they could, accepted as many flowers as they could carry and thanked everyone they met. Women in the crowd wept openly at the sight of the two boys, now faced with the prospect of burying their mother.

And yet both William and Harry behaved with a maturity of which Diana would have been proud, even blushing at unforced applause from the crowd who were taken aback by the remarkably relaxed demeanour of the two boys. At times, people shouted, 'We love you,' and 'God bless you,' and William and Harry waved as a mark of appreciation for the kind sentiments. Then it was time to go and a royal car arrived to whisk them away to St James's Palace, Charles's London home, where they would be staying the night before the funeral. Onlookers on the Mall saw the royal car and the two boys inside and as the car swept slowly by, the crowds cheered and applauded. In their hands, William and Harry held a single white lily, the traditional symbol of death.

The following morning, William awoke early and immediately turned on the television to see what was happening on the streets of London where, in a few hours, the cortège bearing his mother's body would slowly wind its way from Kensington Palace to Westminster Abbey. William watched television pictures of the tens of thousands of people who had braved the cold of a September night to camp out, determined to get a good vantage point from which they could witness Diana's final journey. William saw men, women and even children who had camped out that night, struggling out of their sleeping bags in the cool, early-morning, grey mist that hung over the capital. Shortly after dawn, those who had kept vigil were joined by hundreds of thousands who had left their homes in the early hours to secure a good position to watch the day's events.

There were no dark suits and black ties along the route the cortège would take; not because the mourners had no respect for Diana but because, in her life, she had dressed like them on so many occasions; in shorts, a sweat shirt, a baseball cap and trainers, showing a healthy disregard for the formality and the pomp and ceremony of royal protocol. But William would dress for his mother's funeral in a dark lounge suit, black tie and white shirt, for that was expected of him. For the two princes, this was not a time for the informality their mother had advocated throughout most of her life.

Prince Charles saw the boys at breakfast and asked once more if they were sure they wanted to join him, Earl Spencer and Prince Philip in walking behind the gun carriage that bore their mother's body. They would walk the mile from St James's Palace along the Mall, through Horse Guards Parade and down Whitehall to Westminster Abbey. William answered his father immediately saying that he and Harry had discussed the idea and they most certainly wanted to walk behind the gun carriage, determined to be a part of the funeral. After breakfast they dressed in their suits and black ties and continued to watch the spectacle unfolding on television.

To accommodate the million or more people who wanted to line the route, it had been decided that instead of leaving from St James's Palace, as originally planned, the cortège would start a further mile away at Kensington Palace, Diana's home for most of her adult life. William and Harry sat spellbound that morning as they watched the TV pictures, showing the antique gun carriage drawn by six black horses and accompanied by nine members of the King's Troop, Royal Horse Artillery, and flanked by a bearer-party of 12

Welsh Guardsmen of the Prince of Wales's Company.

William was watching the reaction of the crowds, many in tears, some throwing white flowers over the coffin which was draped in a Royal Standard. There were cries of 'God bless you' and 'We love you' but, for the most part, there was a tense silence, broken only by the sound of people crying openly in their grief. Many hugged each other for comfort, desperate to be consoled, others gripped handkerchiefs and tissues and stood holding them to their faces, alternatively wiping away their tears and choking back the emotion that had overwhelmed them.

William, Harry, Charles, Earl Spencer and Prince Philip gathered in St James's Palace waiting for the moment when they would leave the protection of the historic building and walk out into the autumn sunshine to take their place behind the cortège. The TV cameras focused on the five men — three generations of royalty — as they stood in silence waiting for the cortège to pass by en route to the Abbey. William and Harry had been advised to keep their heads down, looking at the ground in front of them, for, in that way, they would not succumb so easily to the pressure and the atmosphere of grief and sorrow all around them. Each step William and Harry took during that mile-long walk was watched by everyone lining the streets, and the millions watching on television. The silence was almost eerie for the two boys — apart from the muffled sound of the horses' hooves pulling the gun carriage, all William and Harry could hear was the quiet sobbing and weeping of the crowds along the route. Somehow, their strength survived the extraordinary ordeal and they managed to reach the Abbey without either shedding a tear.

Later, William would confess that the funeral service was almost a blur, save for two memorable events; one was the extraordinary, courageous tribute that Earl Spencer made to his sister, and the other was Elton John's rewritten version of 'Candle in the Wind', which Elton had altered to 'Goodbye, England's Rose'. Indeed, the only time that William appeared to be fighting back the tears that welled in his eyes was during Earl Spencer's tribute in which he pledged, in Diana's memory, to protect her two 'beloved sons' from the anguish and tearful despair caused by the paparazzi.

'William and Harry,' Earl Spencer said, addressing them personally from the pulpit, 'we all care desperately for you today. We are all chewed up with the sadness at the loss of a woman who was not even our mother. How great your suffering is, we cannot even imagine.'

William looked up during the last few paragraphs of his tribute, watching anxiously to see whether his uncle would break down, torn apart by the emotion he felt for his elder sister Diana. William could tell that Earl Spencer's voice kept breaking, that he was struggling to complete his speech, the words sticking in his throat as he fought to stop the tears. And William looked around the Abbey when he heard the cheers and applause outside in the streets at the end of Earl Spencer's hard-hitting tribute, the applause reaching a remarkable crescendo as hundreds of thousands of people gave their support to Earl Spencer's promise to continue 'the imaginative and loving way in which you were steering these two exceptional young men, so that their souls are not simply immersed by duty and tradition but can sing openly as you planned.'

And William shared a look with Harry as the 2,000 people in the Abbey, 500 of them representatives of Diana's favourite charities, took up the cheers and began applauding. William knew that no one ever applauds at funerals, especially at funerals of such magnitude, and he looked confused when he realised that the cheers had even been taken up by those privileged to be in the cloistered confines of Westminster Abbey for they had found it impossible to ignore the urge to applaud. Not sure whether he, too, should join in, William, followed by Harry, finally decided that he wanted to applaud, and a smile crept across his face as he found himself eagerly clapping his uncle's tribute, not caring if he was breaking the strict rules of protocol or not.

After Diana's coffin had been borne from

the Abbey to the hearse outside, the Royal Family trooped out to a fleet of waiting cars. Some cars took the Queen, Prince Philip and other members of the Royal Family to Northolt for their flight back to Aberdeen and the seclusion of Balmoral Castle. But Prince Charles, Earl Spencer, Diana's sisters Jane and Sarah and Diana's mother, Frances Shand Kydd, along with William and Harry, took their cars to the railway station for the journey to Althorp, the Spencer family home in Northamptonshire, the place where Diana had grown up. Television cameras were banned for the private burial service on an island in the middle of an oval lake in the grounds of Althorp House.

William and Harry stood around the grave with other members of Diana's family waiting for the cortège, which had been delayed by more than an hour due to the crowds that surged into the path of the hearse and its police escort during the 80-mile journey from London. The vicar from the local church and six pallbearers accompanied the coffin from the hearse to the grave and the two boys watched as the coffin was slowly lowered into the ground. Prayers were said, holy water was sprinkled on the coffin and, within ten minutes, the ceremony was over. William and Harry saw their mother laid to rest and the two lads walked with their father and uncle to Althorp House for tea and sandwiches. An hour later, the two boys, accompanied by their father, drove to Highgrove in Gloucestershire where they arrived in time for dinner.

Their rooms had been prepared, their clothes had been taken by car from London, but neither William nor Harry were ready for bed. One of the longest days in their young lives had seemed to contain so much emotion that they wanted to savour the memories, to go over everything that had occurred that day; the weeping mourners, their mother's cortège, the service in the abbey and the final moments when they saw their mother laid to rest in her grave at Althorp. But shortly after 10.30pm that evening, persuaded by their father, they did finally go to their beds.

Sunday, 7 September dawned bright and sunny and Charles decided that his sons should get out and about rather than staying at home with their memories. Tiggy Legge-Bourke had also travelled to Highgrove and she and Charles determined, without fuss or haste, to encourage William and Harry to look to the future, to the forthcoming school year, to their sporting activities and to once again meeting their pals back at boarding school. Though both boys should have started the new term later that week, it was decided they would stay at Highgrove with Charles and Tiggy, relaxing and getting used to their new life, one without their beloved mother. Those few days went well and both William and Harry enjoyed the outdoors with Tiggy and their father. They would go for walks together, go horse riding and swimming and Tiggy would play football with them in the garden. Charles asked the cook to give the boys their favourite foods, to spoil them in any way they wanted, to make them feel they were precious and wanted and loved.

Charles made sure his sons were never alone during those days of coming to terms with their mother's death and everything that had happened. He involved them in everything, encouraged them to get out and do whatever they wanted and spent most of the time with them. If he wasn't around, then Tiggy would always be present, not permitting them to feel lonely or unloved. William, in particular, sought the presence of his father during those five days. It was as though he felt lost and needed someone to lean on as a bulwark against the world, as a haven of safety, of protection, someone who had the power to guard against all the evils of the world, and especially against the horror of death. William would talk to his father about the car crash, asking him questions which for him had not been satisfactorily answered by the television pundits nor by the newspapers which still wrote daily of the facts that were being unearthed surrounding the details of the accident. William wanted to know who should take the blame for the death of his mother, though he continued to lay most of the blame on the tabloid press and the scavaging photographers.

Before the following weekend, both boys

said they were happy and fully prepared to return to their respective schools; William to Eton and Harry to Ludgrove. For William, however, there was also a feeling of guilt, a twinge of conscience that he was leaving Harry to fight his own corner when William knew that his mother had always asked him to protect his younger brother. Ever since the car crash, William had been behaving more like a parent towards Harry than an older brother, in keeping with what he believed his mother would have wanted and thoroughly approved of. Indeed, ever since William and Harry had been told of the death of their mother, William had been at pains hardly ever to let Harry out of his sight. William spoke to his father and to Tiggy about this predicament and his sense of guilt, and they both assured him that, once back at school, Harry would be fine. They also assured him that if Harry needed to phone William, then the headmaster would understand and allow him to do so at any time.

For Harry, it would be his final year at Ludgrove before he, too, would join his brother at Eton in September 1998. Both William and

Harry were, reportedly, happy to be back at school, their daily lives full of lessons, activities, sports events and the rough and tumble of boarding school life, helping them to get over the tragedy that had struck so hard and so swiftly. William, in particular, enjoyed being back with his close friends all of whom had been told that, after offering their condolences to William over the death of his mother, to refrain from discussing or mentioning the matter unless he wanted to talk about it. And, as before, the daily newspapers were first scrutinised by a master before being handed to William, in case they contained any offensive or upsetting articles. In fact, the daily chore had no real effect because William was able to see any newspaper he wanted, any day he wished, simply by going into Windsor and buying one. However, no matter how tempted he may have been, it is understood that he never read the newspapers at that time, mainly because his mother had always warned him against what the papers wrote about the Royal Family. Diana had always believed the tabloids usually wrote inaccurate, offensive rubbish which had no bearing on the true facts.

William was relieved to be back in the protective atmosphere of Eton among his friends. He loved the anonymity of Eton life where no one paid him any special attention; where he could chat and relax and have fun with his pals like any other boy. It was all so very different from the overbearing glare of the spotlight that he had faced during the funeral. And William loathes the public limelight, hates being the centre of attention, for it always forcefully reminds him of the treatment his mother often suffered at the hands of the photographers and the tabloid press.

Indeed, William came through the ordeal of his mother's death and highly public funeral with flying colours, surprising everyone who knew of his natural enmity towards the press and personal publicity. In her life, Diana had tried to persuade William that the cameras and press attention were a necessary evil of his life and that he had to learn to live with them. William knew that his mother would have expected him to behave with maturity and equanimity towards the cameras on this most public occasion and that was probably one of the reasons he surprised everyone with his calmness, sense of responsibility and his acceptance of routine traditional duty.

12

The People's Prince

Christmas 1997 was, of course, a very difficult, if not traumatic, time for both William and Harry and, indeed, for the entire Royal Family. The family all realised that they had to handle the festive season in a delicate, unobtrusive way, making sure they did not ignore the fact that Diana was no longer around but also trying to make sure William and Harry enjoyed themselves, never allowing them to lapse into sentimental feelings of loneliness and grief which would only hinder their efforts to come to terms with their mother's death.

For most of the time, Charles, aided by Tiggy and their cousin Peter Phillips, did manage, for the most part, to make Sandringham a laughter-filled, happy, environment for William and Harry. But their mother was not forgotten. When they all went to church on Christmas Day, prayers were offered for the repose of the soul of Diana, Princess of Wales, and William was happy that his mother was still at the forefront of their minds. Nonetheless Christmas 1997 was a difficult time for William and he missed his mother terribly but, despite the feeling of loss, he put a brave face on the proceedings, mainly for the sake of Harry who seemed to be racing around Sandringham, getting on with his favourite pursuits.

Throughout the Christmas holiday, however, William could never forget those last few Christmases following the official separation of his parents. Those times had been tough for him. He knew that his mother was staying on her own in London while he and Harry accompanied their father to

Sandringham for the Royal Family's traditional Christmas get-together. William recalled that those Christmases at Sandringham had not been fun, in fact the very opposite. He remembered the times he had talked to his mother on the phone and how sad he had felt, sensing her unhappiness, knowing that she was missing him and Harry so much that she was near to tears. He recalled the times when he tried to be brave, keeping a stiff upper lip, but had often cried himself to sleep at night in the solitude and secrecy of his bed. William knew that no one had realised how awful those days had been for him; for most of the time, he only wanted to be with his mother, hoping that she was all right, that she wasn't too sad at being parted from her sons.

Those days also made him feel isolated and helpless because he could do nothing to rectify the situation. He understood that his father and other members of the Royal Family tried to make amends, tried to create a happy, fun-filled atmosphere at Christmas for him and Harry as well as the other young royals who came to stay. But he had found it difficult to laugh, to enjoy himself or to join in the enthusiastic games and Christmas festivities.

As a result, William was more than happy to return to the chummy atmosphere of Eton, to be once again amongst his friends where he could relax and concentrate on school work, games and the everyday hurly-burly of school life. But Christmas 1997 had been by far the worst time of all. It wasn't that the Royal Family had been anything but kind, considerate and understanding throughout the holidays. It was simply the fact that being amongst them reminded him every waking moment of the day of the death of his beloved mother; and every time he thought of her, tears came to his eyes.

For six months following Diana's funeral, William didn't make one public appearance and, as a result of the battering the tabloids were given by the British people following Diana's death, no photographs and very few newspaper articles were written about either William or Harry. The newspapers had finally backed off, giving the young princes the peace which they needed to come to terms with their mother's death. William knew in his heart that the tabloids and the paparazzi had gone away because they realised that they were partly responsible for the tragedy. In his tribute to Diana, her brother Earl Spencer said, 'There is no doubt that she was looking for a new direction in her life at the time of her death. She talked endlessly of getting away from England, mainly because of the treatment that she received at the hands of the newspapers. I don't think she ever understood why her genuinely good intentions were sneered at by the media, why there appeared to be a permanent quest on their behalf to bring her down.'

William had not realised that his mother intended to move abroad, leaving him and Harry behind, but he did understand the appalling, disgraceful pressure she was put under every time she appeared in public. William understood that his mother could not travel anywhere in Britain, whether to the shops, the gym, the cinema or out to dinner without half-a-dozen paparazzi dogging her every step and snapping away with their cameras, sometimes making it difficult for her to walk down a street as they poked their cameras within inches of her face, determined to get as close as possible to their victim. In fact, Diana was not contemplating leaving William and Harry behind. She was searching for a home abroad where she could live in peace and comfort, a place hidden from the public gaze or the prying lenses of cameramen where she could escape to during term times when William and Harry were away at school and, more importantly, a home where William and Harry could stay happily with her during their school holidays.

But Earl Spencer's scathing attacks on the British tabloids achieved the required objective for his views were backed by the vast majority of the British people. The tabloid proprietors and editors knew that if they hounded and pestered Diana's young sons in the way they had hounded their mother, the British public would react with such anger that newspaper circulations would suffer, hitting them where it hurt most, in their pockets. As a result, the Press Complaints Commission —

the body charged with enforcing the code of practice for editors to follow — met in urgent session after Diana's death, to consider what changes they should make to the rules governing press intrusion.

Journalists, photographers, television cameramen and anyone associated with the media had been given a rough ride by the public for their perceived role in the accident in Paris. 'Scum' was the word often heard during those days following her death, a sentiment which William agreed with entirely.

Three weeks after Diana's funeral, Lord Wakeham, Chairman of the Press Complaints Commission, issued a statement in which he outlined a new, stricter code for the media to follow. He dealt with harassment of individuals, especially famous people and members of the Royal Family. He proposed that the industry should prohibit the publication of pictures obtained through 'persistent pursuit or as a result of "unlawful behaviour".' And he tried to control the practice of freelance paparazzi photographers being used by newspapers to obtain 'exclusive' pictures, demanding that the picture agencies who employ the paparazzi sign up to the Code of Practice. And in a bid to protect William and Harry, as well as other children of famous parents, Lord Wakeham said newspapers could have no excuse for invading the privacy of a child because the press should recognise the particularly vulnerable position of children whose parents are in the public eye.

As a result, newspapers, television cameramen and even the great majority of freelance paparazzi photographers kept away from William and Harry following Diana's death, not daring to risk the anger of readers and viewers trying to win back the respect of the nation. More importantly, the newspaper owners and chairmen of television companies ordered their editors to lay off the young princes. However, one or two paparazzi did tail William and his pals when they ventured from Eton into Windsor to go shopping or have a tea or coffee in the town. Some photographers took long lens shots of William rowing on the Thames, but although those pictures were offered to Britain's tabloid editors, none of them bought or published the shots. Such pictures did, however, sometimes make their way into American and European newspapers and magazines.

But young William was growing up fast. The first signs that William was becoming a cult figure, perhaps even an object of lustful desire among the teenage generation, was in November 1997 when he attended a lunch at the Royal Naval College in Greenwich, celebrating his grandparents' 50th wedding anniversary. Six hundred screaming teenage girls heralded his arrival much to the surprise of everyone else attending the lunch. No one had seen such a reaction to the youthful William's appearance before, and even the police were taken aback for no one was expecting such an ardent reception. In fact, the first signs that Prince William might become a target for teenage passion occurred two years earlier, in October 1995, when the pop magazine *Smash Hits* published a poster of a boyish William dressed in an uncool blazer, tie and grey trousers. It was a sell out. Five months later, William received 54

Valentine cards, and a year later he had more than 500. In 1998 he received more than 1,000!

But the photographs of William taken during his visit to Canada in March 1998, still came as a great surprise to the British people. The young, somewhat shy, modest, even bashful boy the world had known had matured into a confident, remarkably handsome and tall young man with a winning smile. Everyone who saw the television pictures, as well as those published in newspapers across the world, immediately drew a comparison with his mother. In Diana's first pictures she, too, had appeared shy and modest, even timid. And what threw many people who saw the handsome William was the physical likeness between Diana and her elder son. Today, William bears a haunting resemblance to his mother, with her engaging smile and fair hair. In fact, William closely resembles his late grandfather, the former Earl Spencer when he was a dashing young army officer, commissioned into the Royal Scots Greys, and who had become an equerry to both King

George VI and to the Queen. In the late 1940s and 1950s, the tall, dashing Johnny Spencer was considered one of the most handsome young men in London Society and invited to all the balls, dances and parties.

During his 1998 visit to Canada with his father and young Harry, William was exposed to the full treatment, the adulation of screaming, lustful teenage girls. He was totally taken aback by the reception the Vancouver girls gave him, screaming at him 'I love you' whenever William appeared in public. At first he did not know how to react to such an enthusiastic reception. When he arrived at Vancouver's Waterfront Centre Hotel on the first evening of the holiday, he looked nervously towards the group of 200 teenage girls screaming for his attention, put his head down and walked briskly into the hotel, disappointing his young fans.

But his father, who had witnessed William's arrival, knew that he had to persuade young William to cope with such events, for he would become the centre of attention no matter what. Charles knew this welcome was only the first of many, perhaps hundreds or thousands of such scenes which would be repeated over the coming years. Prince Charles knew that William and Harry would have to face a far sterner test than he ever had to endure in his youth. Charles recognised that in the past 30 years, teenagers had become far more open, transparent and expressive about their sexual desires, which they usually reserve for pop stars and actors. But William touched a chord in the hearts of Vancouver's young women, for he is unique. He is not only a royal prince, heir to the British throne, but he is also a handsome, good-looking young man, and the son of Princess Diana who had become an icon across the western world.

That evening in Vancouver, Charles talked to William, explaining that this was his first great test following his remarkably mature presence at the time of his mother's death. Charles explained that being a royal prince, a member of the House of Windsor and heir to the British throne, meant that appearing in public was one of the duties he would have to face and get used to. Charles understood that

William hated the press and, in particular, the paparazzi and the tabloid photographers, but Charles explained that he and Harry would have to learn to live with photographers because they would be a part of their lives, for ever.

The following morning, Charles, William and Harry made a private visit to the Pacific Space Centre in Vancouver, but somehow the young girls had learned of the visit and 200 waited to see their Prince Charming. As the visit was private, the girls only managed to catch a fleeting glimpse of their new idol but the screams of hysteria could be heard throughout the building.

William would later be greeted by even more wild adulation and even louder screams when he visited Burnaby South Secondary School in Vancouver. The manic screaming was like nothing William had ever faced before, with 300 teenage girls, tears streaming down their cheeks, desperate to shake William's hand or simply to touch him.

'William, William, William,' they screamed as the young prince walked towards them, smiling broadly, as though he had enjoyed such experiences many times before. William was learning fast.

In a matter of days, he had learned to cope with the screaming adulation and act as if such receptions were an everyday event. This time he stood his ground, smiled like a professional and seemed in command of the situation, happily shaking the hands of his young adolescent admirers, accepting their gifts of cuddly toys, dodging the daffodils the girls threw towards him, pressing the flesh like a Hollywood star. The screams, the tears, and the fever pitch of excitement, reminiscent of the adulation showered on pop stars, had been a revelation to him. And yet, in a matter of a few hours, William had learned how to cope with such strident acclamation. When a group of girls were asked why they found William so appealing, attractive and desirable, one answered, 'He's rich, he's gorgeous and he's a prince. What more do you need?'

But the *pièce de résistance* came during the last official stop of the visit at the heritage centre on the Vancouver waterfront. The main event was supposed to be a speech by Prince Charles, but the 500 girls who turned up had other ideas. Struggling for breath between sobs, screams and near-hysteria, the girls offered William flowers, teddy bears, tear-stained handkerchiefs and eternal love. William strolled from one group to another, smiling, shaking hands and saying 'Thank you' to one and all in exactly the same way as his mother had done a thousand times during her lifetime.

On this occasion, however, William even behaved like his mother, looking slightly bashful, ill-at-ease and shy like any teenager would have done when faced with such unbridled teenage passion. Then, unexpectedly and dramatically, William completely stole the occasion. After accepting a gift of a baseball jacket and 'poor boy' cap, William shook off his own jacket and slipped into his new clothes — cap peak at the back of course — and then twirled and gave a rap-style roll of the wrist and shoulders. His bit of fun had been spontaneous; no one in the royal party was aware that William was planning any such gesture. Indeed, due to his natural antipathy towards the cameras the photographers and television crews were unprepared, taken aback by his behaviour. The audience, however, was delirious, the crescendo of cheering adoration almost deafening.

During that moment, Prince William seemed to enjoy the limelight for the first time in his life. He also seemed blissfully unaware of the TV cameras and the photographers who clicked away madly as they scrambled between themselves to get pictures of the world's newest superstar. 'Willsmania' had arrived.

And neither was Prince Harry forgotten in the mayhem. Though Harry was only 13, a number of the girls wanted to shake his hand and touch him but not with the same raw passion as they showed towards William. Indeed, Harry thoroughly enjoyed the occasion, goading his elder brother into moving from one group of admirers to another so he could see the hysterical reaction his big brother caused. Harry was laughing at the girls' responses and urged William to continue his new-found role as the great attraction of the Royal House of Windsor.

For his part, Prince Charles looked on with admiration, fully realising that here indeed the Royal Family had a new star who commanded such attention and adulation. But Charles, who had also been the centre of media attention during his early years, realised that he would have to ration William's appearances to enable his son to concentrate on his education, his exams and his future role. The extraordinary scenes, however, did much to enliven the royal visit to Canada which was really meant to be a private skiing holiday for the three of them rather than a baptism of fire for William. For the greater part of this trip, the TV cameramen and the photographers left the royal party in peace, happily cutting a deal for a single photo-opportunity on the ski slopes before agreeing to leave them entirely alone to enjoy their holiday.

During that skiing holiday, there was one wonderful, spontaneous moment which somewhat embarrassed Prince Charles and his sons. After one morning's skiing was over, the three walked into a mountain café for a bite to eat. Nothing had been planned and no one had any idea that Charles, William and Harry would turn up to eat at that particular establishment. However, as soon as they were recognised, the 300 skiers enjoying their lunch rose to their feet as one and applauded the royal party. That standing ovation was entirely spontaneous, a sign of the warmth Canadians feel towards the British Royal Family, and the moment cheered Charles.

The holiday was a tonic for Charles and his sons and getting away from Britain for a week to enjoy the sun and the snow helped to forge a closer bond between the three of them. It was the first time William and Harry had been alone with their father since the traumatic days following their mother's death. This was a holiday together and the three of them appeared to be very much at ease with each other, as though they had discovered a new, deeper relationship. No longer would William and Harry have to juggle their affections towards one or other of their parents; no longer would they be forced to decide whether they wanted to spend weekends or holidays with their father or mother; no longer would they feel compelled to take sides, supporting one against the other; and no longer would there be an atmosphere fraught with friction as the boys floated between their parents' homes.

In particular, William had discovered a new role model, his own father. Now, at the age of 18, William understands more than anyone the strains and pressures that have been placed upon his father as heir to the throne. Charles knows the problems that hero-worship will bring to his son, as he is also aware that the British press has a nasty habit of building up the nation's heroes only to revel in knocking them down at a later stage. Charles will do his utmost to protect his sons but he knows that in William's case he has the added problem of advising and guiding a potential superstar. Charles is also aware that William will find it far easier thwarting the lustful desires of young 14- and 15-year-olds than the 20-somethings who will soon find the handsome, good-looking young William irresistible, a target for their more focused demands and sexual ambitions.

The question that every teenage girl now wants answered is exactly what kind of young man William is. What's he *really* like? Well, many are rather surprised when they meet him. At first he is shy and bashful, self-effacing and sometimes awkward. But that is only a protective shell behind which he hides whenever he meets new people or a fresh situation. He has every reason to be guarded for he trusts no one on sight. He knows that many will tell tales about him, sell stories to the tabloids and, if necessary, sell him down the river. So, William puts up his guard and only slowly permits people to become close to him. He will surreptiously watch strangers who have entered his circle, trying to calculate whether he should trust them or blank them. It is a problem that few 19-year-old teenagers have to think about but to William it is incredibly important. As a result, young William has had to mature faster than the average teenager and those adults who meet and chat to him describe him as seeming two or three years older than his actual age.

Within a few years, there will be a number of mothers who will soon be debating the identity of the young woman that Prince William will one day marry. The tabloid press will throw up a few names but, generally speaking, they have no real idea of the social life of the heir to the throne.

Most people believe that young William has the character, personality and natural gifts of his mother; that in his maturity he will have the same gentle touch, the same spontaneous reaction to those less fortunate; the same compassion, a symbol of selfless humanity coupled with a sense of duty and a natural nobility. He also has considerable sex appeal. From now on, his public appearances are likely to evoke a voracious public interest, more enthusiastic, more hysterical and more frenzied than those that greeted his mother. In some ways, it does appear that the young are transferring their adoration of Diana to William; and the women who threw their support behind Diana and her troubled life, also seem to want to do all they can to support both William and Harry. But at least William is better prepared to deal with public acclaim than Diana ever was. William has been born into royalty, trained to understand his role and the part he will play. Already, the signs are there that William will become the person that Diana hoped he would, a people's prince.

13

William, the Man

William was not best pleased with his 'A' level examination results because he only achieved an 'A' in Geography, a 'B' in History of Art and a lowly 'C' in Biology. He was confident that he had done better than that and was disappointed because he had worked hard and had done better in his mocks.

Even before his 'A' levels, William had been thinking of trying for a place at St Andrews in Scotland because he wanted to be as far away as possible from paparazzi photographers and Fleet Street reporters. At St Andrews, William would also be quite near Balmoral — about 120 miles by road — and he rather liked the idea of being able to escape to the peace and quiet of Balmoral where he could shoot, ride horses and fish in the River Dee.

He also believed that at St Andrews he would be more out of the limelight compared to life at Oxford or Cambridge. Prince Charles went to Trinity College, Cambridge, but he was able to lead a secluded, sheltered life, untroubled by voracious gangs of photographers and tabloid reporters. William fully realised that even if the British tabloids agreed not to hassle William during his university years he knew full well that both photographers and reporters from American and the sensational European newspapers and magazines were likely to think the heir to the throne was fair game now he was over nineteen years of age and an adult.

William went to St Andrews and chatted with members of staff who took him on a tour of the university, explaining the layout of the place and the problems he might face from uninvited intruders, like the press. He talked of St Andrews having a relaxed atmosphere which he felt would suit his personality.

Finally, William decided that he would be happier at St Andrews. He felt there would be less pressure and he hoped the students whom he would meet and live with during his four-year course would be more friendly, more approachable and less stuffy and snooty than those he might meet at Oxford or Cambridge. Prince Charles also visited St Andrews, but he let William reach his own decision.

It seems most likely that after St Andrews, William, who will then be twenty-three years old, will want to join the Army. He has said on numerous occasions that he would like to join the armed forces and he has always shown a preference for the army.

He might, however, like his father before him, learn to fly with the RAF and then move to the Royal Navy. Only time will tell.

In his five years at Eton, William has forged close relationships with half-a-dozen boys of his own age. He gets on well with them all and they, in turn, treat him no differently to other boys at the school. He loves that. He is known for his sense of fun, his engaging smile, his relaxed attitude and his determination to succeed, whether at sport or academically. William has fitted in very well at Eton, has thrived in the culture of the school which has a reputation of being able to absorb all kinds of boys from different backgrounds and encourage them to become confident, outgoing young men who know they are a breed apart. The school also encourages all the boys to work hard and expects them to excel in whatever area they chose, whether it is languages, classics, science or sculling, playing squash or football. William, it seems, is enjoying not only the camaraderie and anonymity of Eton but also the academic and sporting challenges the school has to offer.

Since the death of his mother, William has become a far more confident young man. And Eton has helped him to relax and enjoy himself far more than when he first arrived at the school, when he appeared to be a shy, introvert and wary teenager, unsure of himself and his capabilities. At first, he felt that the other boys at Eton were more intelligent than him and he worked hard to prove himself. Academically, William has done well and is certainly one of the most conscientious boys in his class. As a result, every exam he has sat, including nine GCSEs, he has passed with ease. He has already proved that he certainly has brains. And he uses them.

William also has brawn. At first, William enjoyed rowing at Eton and in the summer term of 1997 he could be seen frequently sculling on the Thames. Such exercise builds great arm, back and leg muscles, and with his natural development William blossomed into a powerful young man for his age. This summer, however, he has been persuaded to switch to swimming, his mother's favourite sport, and he has proved an exceptional talent. His upper body strength and athletic physique has propelled William into Britain's top 100 swimmers for his age in the 50-metre freestyle. In March 1998, he won Eton's junior 100-metre and 50-metre freestyle and clocked the fastest time since 1987 at the Berkshire

County schools finals.

If William decided to train with a professional coach, Britain's Amateur Swimming Association spokesmen believe the heir to the throne could become a serious challenger for national honours. But that would involve strict and tough practice sessions, swimming at least twice a day, every day, with his own personal trainer. It may be that William would like to accept that challenge, following in the footsteps of his aunt Princess Anne who represented Britain in three-day eventing at the Olympics, as well as his hero Peter Phillips who played rugby for Scotland.

William is undoubtedly a natural athlete. He enjoys a number of sports including rowing, football and water polo. He has played rugby but doesn't enjoy that winter sport as much as soccer in which he has shown real talent. William also plays tennis and squash, two sports in which he has shown quite exceptional talent, with his tall, powerful build giving him an advantage over boys of his own age. He is also a competent skier and has become quite a daredevil on the slopes, now outpacing his father on some of the most difficult off-piste slopes at Klosters in Switzerland, Aspen, in Colorado, USA, and in Canada. He loves the challenge of racing downhill.

And, of course, there are personal challenges involved in the country pursuits which he has enjoyed with his father and Tiggy. In all these he has revealed a keen interest and competence as well as a determination to compete and prove himself. He is now a better shot than Tiggy and she was always considered very competent. One of the reasons William has proved such a natural talent at most sports is because of the competitive side of his nature which belies the image he portrays in public. People simply do not realise how determined, earnest and resolute William can be when playing sports. He likes to win. He believes that he must prove himself to a greater extent than any of his contemporaries, simply because of his position, the son of the Prince of Wales. He asks for no quarter and gives none in any sport. He also reveals a stubborness, refusing to be beaten, never giving up even when the situation looks hopeless. In the team games William plays he shows a great capacity for encouraging others, one of the reasons he was made captain of Ludgrove's first football XI. He is seen as a natural leader.

In the privacy of his room at Eton, as well as his bedroom at home, Wills loved to shut himself away and listen to rock music, so very different from the classical and opera music which his father prefers. William would walk around with his Walkman listening to loud, hard rock music oblivious to everyone around him. The British band Pulp were one his great favourites. He had also been smitten by the Spice Girls, and loved their raunchy music.

And he knows how to dress. In the American *People* magazine's Best Dressed People of 1996, the editors wrote, 'He looks and dresses like a model. He makes no mistakes.' And William's dress sense covers every facet of his life, whether he is dressing in classical English tweeds and brogues with his father, designer T-shirts, jeans and sneakers when wearing casual apparel, or dressing with style and colour when skiing. Of course, William had his elegant mother to advise him. It remains to be seen whether he will now develop his own inimitable style, coupled with good taste and a knack of always looking great in whatever he wears.

Shortly before William left Eton in the summer of 2000, Prince Charles had a long talk to his son during a walk they were taking with the dogs at Highgrove. On numerous occasions during the previous year, Charles had chatted to him about his future plans, wanting to learn what he would like to do after leaving Eton. Charles recognised that nothing definite could be finalised until they were certain that William had passed his 'A'-levels with grades high enough to be accepted at Oxford, Cambridge or any other university.

But on this occasion, Charles wanted to discuss with William the sensitive matter of girls.

Charles began by explaining to William that, unlike every other young man, he would always be in a difficult situation simply because he was the heir to the throne and a member of the House of Windsor. Charles emphasised that because he was the grandson of the Queen, he would have to deal with relationships in a totally different way to all his friends and acquaintances. Charles was aware that William knew all about the facts of life because Tiggy had told him that William was well 'clued up' and needed no further sex education. In any case, the matter of sex, contraception and relationships had been dealt with in a full and open way at Eton.

His father told William that he was well aware that the young women of today were far more open and far more forward than in his own younger days in the late 1960s and early 1970s.

As a result, Charles believed that William would have a far more difficult task coping with sexually aggressive, amorous and adventurous young women than he ever experienced in his youth.

William would confess to friends later that he believed the delicate conversation had gone quite well but he felt his father was a little embarrassed at having to go into so much detail. William also told his friends that he was aware of many potential problems that his father touched on, but he respected the fact that Charles had discussed the matter with him in a straightforward, man-to-man way.

Charles also told William that, if he wished, he could take the advice that Lord Mountbatten had given him when he was a young man. Charles's great-uncle, who had always been closer to Charles than Prince Philip, advised Charles, 'I believe in a case like yours, the heir to the throne, a young man should sow his wild oats and have as many affairs as he can before settling down.'

On another occasion, Mountbatten had told Charles that when the time came to settle down, he should find a suitable young virgin, marry her and quickly produce some heirs for the next generation. Prince Charles had taken that advice despite the fact that he was never a natural womaniser unlike his own father, Prince Philip. Indeed, many of the girls he openly dated and whom the tabloid press made a fuss over, were never more than friends.

Charles told William that he hoped he would have the same relationship with him that he had enjoyed with Mountbatten. To all intents and purposes, Mountbatten had taken the role of surrogate father as well as his principal adviser on every step in his career. Charles told his son how, at every turn, he had sought out Mountbatten's counsel. When on leave from the Royal Navy, Charles would nearly always visit his great-uncle at his home at Broadlands in Hampshire. They would sit and chat or go for a walk together. Charles had loved and cherished the relationship and Charles found that Broadlands, where he was always welcomed by his cheery, smiling, ebullient great-uncle became a much-needed home to him.

Charles explained to William that unfortunately he had never really enjoyed a home life at any time during his childhood days. His memories were of being brought up by maids and nannies and as a result, he had always yearned for life in a home in which everyone sat down to meals together, enjoyed their weekends together, the children chatting with their parents at any time of the day. Charles explained to William how he had always felt distant from his parents. He explained how he had been brought up in awe of his mother, and his father hadn't been as actively involved with him as he might have liked.

And Charles impressed on William that Highgrove would always be an open house for him and for Harry, a place to bring their friends, whether school pals or girlfriends. He told William that it was his dearest wish that the two of them should enjoy the same sort of relationship and close bond that had existed between him and his great-uncle. He also told William of the terrible distress he suffered when Earl Mountbatten was murdered by the IRA when holidaying in Ireland in 1979.

At the conclusion of that long, intimate conversation, in which his father had explained what his upbringing had been like 30 years earlier, William was a very happy young man. His father had often chatted to William about a hundred and one different matters, particularly following the death of his mother. But this chat, as they walked together through the winter countryside dressed in Barbours, heavy sweaters, warm trousers and green wellies, had been the most open conversation they had ever enjoyed. William felt that his father had spoken to him as an adult and taken him into his confidence. Later, William would say that his father had made him feel more grown up, more mature, more prepared to face the outside world after the sheltered atmosphere of Eton.

In some ways, however, William's chat with his father about sexual matters had come as quite a surprise. Wills had never expected his father to be so open and forward-thinking towards sexual matters. William had come to believe that he would have to keep his girlfriends away from Highgrove, away from his father, because he feared Charles would frown on having William's girlfriends visit Highgrove. William had thought it might have been fine to invite a girl over for coffee or a meal, but he had never thought for one minute that his father would permit a girl to stay over. William still wasn't certain however, that when push came to shove, his father would ever let him sleep with a girl unless things were really serious between them. He decided that he would just take things slowly and see what happened when he did invite a girl over. He decided to start by inviting girls over for coffee, a meal or to a barbecue and see how that went down with his father before risking anything further. But the prospect excited him.

William and a couple of his Eton friends had a great laugh discussing the sexual implications of Charles's chat. They all wondered if their parents would really let them bring girls to their homes and let them sleep together or whether they would have to pretend to sleep in different rooms. They discussed what their parents would really say to them when they asked whether it was OK to bring a girlfriend back home to stay the night. The three teenagers wondered at what age they would be allowed to ask girls to stop over and they also wondered at what age it was OK to ask girls to spend the night. They all confessed that they had no idea what the girls' parents might say at such a suggestion. The two other boys said they intended to speak to their parents and put forward the same suggestion to them. They planned to use the chat William had enjoyed with his father to suggest that they should be permitted the same privilege. They all agreed it had been 'brilliant' of Prince Charles to adopt such a modern outlook on sex and totally agreed with the advice he had given William.

Until that chat with his father, William had never thought there would be a possibility of bringing girls back home. He had always thought that his mother might have permitted girls to stay over at Kensington Palace because she was so much younger and less inhibited and more understanding than his father. He had believed that his mother would have understood that it was better to invite girls to stay the night or a weekend at Kensington Palace rather than having him stay at some pal's home where he could secretly enjoy a night with a girlfriend. But for his father to entertain the same ideas had amazed him. He decided to keep his fingers crossed and hope for the best.

Most of William's conversations with his father over the past couple of years concerned duty, William's duty in his role as heir to the throne and as a member of the House of Windsor. And Charles pulled no punches, letting William know that he had a tough life ahead of him. Charles had explained to him that there was no easy road ahead for William but, in contrast, his brother Harry would have only a few of the duties compared to the number William would have to bear.

Charles explained that in one way William was very fortunate to have been born into the Royal Family but, he pointed out, that the hard work, the pressure, the constant demands on his life and his time totally outweighed the privileges. Charles would sometimes almost frighten William when he explained what lay ahead of him.

Throughout these conversations, Charles would instil in William the essence of his future life — duty. His father told him that duty would be paramount throughout his life and he must never forget that fact. Above all, there was duty to the Royal Family and the monarchy; there was duty to the British people and those of the Commonwealth; and also duty to the Establishment, the Church, the Government and politicians. All these people and institutions had to be treated with graciousness and the greatest respect, purely and simply because it would be William's duty to do so.

And Charles explained that his son's life would never be his own. His diary would be completed for him, detailing precisely where he had to be and at what time and on what date. His private secretary would tell him whom he would meet, what he would say and for how long he would be able to talk. His life would be run like a railway timetable, only in William's case there would never be any excuses for being late on any occasion.

Charles warned William that initially his life would seem very interesting but that after the first few years of attending the same functions, meeting the same people and having the same conversations it would rapidly become something of a bore. It was on those occasions that he would have to remind himself that it was his duty to concentrate, appear animated and interested. It would be one of his tasks to indulge people at all times and on all occasions. Not for one moment could he ever appear disinterested or indifferent on any subject, no matter if inwardly he felt the whole meeting tedious and boring in the extreme. He had to pretend and show that he was fascinated.

And he had to learn how to handle people, make them feel at ease, joke kindly with them and help them to relax. Charles told him that no matter how nervous he felt on some occasions, he could guarantee that the person he was meeting would be far more nervous. That made William laugh.

And Charles explained that many of the meetings he attended, many of the people he would have to talk to or sit next to at an official lunch would talk about matters and events that William would find completely boring. But on those occasions, Charles told him, he would have to understand that he would have to pretend the conversation was scintillating or, at the very least, interesting. Neither would he be able to speak his own mind either in conversations or meetings.

Indeed, Charles told him that officially William would not be permitted any personal views except among his own tight family group. He would never be able to make his personal views known nor comment on any government or council decisions or policies. In all political matters of any elected bodies or institutions, he would have to be absolutely neutral, no matter if he did have any views of his own, political or otherwise. In many respects, Charles told him, being heir to the throne was like being a political neuter.

Charles also explained that William would have very little say in ordering his own life except in one particular area. And that was the choice of the young woman he would want to marry.

And once again, Charles took his son into his confidence. Charles had told various close friends, as well as one or two senior advisers, that he was determined never to treat his sons in the way he had been treated by his father. Charles explained to William that from the age of 27 his father had suggested, every month or so, that it was about time he found a wife, got married and produced some heirs. Charles told William that it wasn't only his father who applied such pressure. Heavy hints were dropped by his mother, Church of England bishops, government ministers, senior members of the aristocracy and even Buckingham Palace courtiers.

He told William that the pressure everyone applied became nearly unbearable with questions being asked whenever the newspapers pictured him with a new girl. It didn't seem to matter whether they were genuine girlfriends or simply friends of friends, but the questions would come thick and fast, everyone wondering if 'this girl' or 'that girl' was the one he intended to marry.

Charles promised William during that conversation that, no matter what happened, he would never put pressure on him to marry any particular person at any time. Charles confessed to his son that the more pressure that was applied to him to marry, the less he had wanted to go through with it. Such pressure had made him feel that it didn't matter whether he loved, or didn't love the girl involved, but that he should marry solely to provide an heir for the House of Windsor to ensure the continuance of the royal line. Charles also told William to report to him anyone in authority who ever tried to push him to marry because he would intervene personally to protect his son's interests.

Charles also discussed the question of drugs with William. His father emphasised that under no circumstances must William ever even think of experimenting with drugs, let alone use them. Charles explained that he understood many teenagers tried drugs and there was a great temptation to experiment, but he pointed out the unbelievable embarrassment that would be caused to the Royal Family if it became public knowledge that William, or indeed Harry, had ever tried drugs. William understood that and told his father that he had contemplated trying cannabis to see what it was like, but had not done so and would not do so. William also told Charles that he was well aware of drugs and of the numbers of young people who experimented and used them.

Throughout William's final hectic year at Eton when he was working hard for his 'A'-level exams and enjoying a variety of sports, Charles also talked to him about his plans after university. For some years, William had told his father that he wanted to take a short service commission in the Army but he wasn't sure which branch of the Army he should join.

William was adamant that he didn't want to join the Household Cavalry or the Brigade of Guards because they were too élitist. He was thinking of joining the Royal Marines, a regiment where the officers and men worked together as a team and which was considered to be one of the toughest and most professional regiments in the British Army. He had once considered joining the SAS, but had dropped that idea because of the potential political risks he could be exposed to when taking part in overseas operations.

Prince Charles explained that he had thoroughly enjoyed his later career in the Royal Navy, although he found it tough at the beginning of his service when he was a junior officer because none of his fellow officers would talk to him. After some years, however, when he had won the trust of other officers, and particularly when given command of his own ship, he loved the camaraderie of the Royal Navy. He warned William that it was very difficult being in such circumstances because none of the other officers knew how to behave towards to the heir to the throne. Some feigned friendship, others didn't dare speak for fear of being rude or saying something out of order. Consequently, Charles said he often felt an embarrassment rather than being accepted as just another officer, part of the ship's company. And in the conversation, Charles warned William that the same might well happen to him if he ever decided to serve in the armed forces.

Despite these warnings, William was still adamant that once he had completed his university studies he did want to spend some years in the Army, perhaps learning to parachute as his father had done during his time in the forces. Charles, of course, during the time he served in the Royal Air Force, also learned to fly supersonic fighter aircraft and helicopters. William told his father that one day he, too, would like to learn to fly aircraft and helicopters. But the Army would remain his first choice.

But before William would have to reach any decision about which of the armed forces he would join, there was the all-important matter of which university he would attend. Diana had discussed with William whether he would be interested in attending university in the United States, perhaps going to Harvard. William liked the idea but he first wanted to visit one to see whether he would fit in or whether he might feel out of place in a university full of American students. But Diana was never able to organise such a visit before the Paris crash.

Charles was keen for his son to go up to Cambridge where he was a student for three years in the late 1960s. Against the advice of his tutors, who believed him capable of a first-class honours degree, Charles opted for a broad education, choosing anthropology and archaeology in his first year, then history in his final two years. Charles chose to spread the subjects in that way because he believed that, as a future King of England, it was his duty to Crown and country to educate himself in a broad range of matters. Charles left Cambridge with a BA honours degree, gaining a respectable 2.2. His tutors believed, however, that if he had not been subjected to interruptions due to his royal heritage (for example, taking a three-month break to learn Welsh at Aberystwyth), he would have earned a better degree.

Prince Charles related all these facts to his son so that he would understand exactly what he had done and the reasons why he had made his decisions. Charles didn't want his son to make the same mistakes. Undoubtedly, Charles has a good mind and is an intelligent man, but he believes that William is showing signs of being more intelligent and Charles wants him to make sure he doesn't waste his natural ability. Having spoken to his tutors at Eton, Charles is of the opinion that William should go for a first-class honours degree and should be quite capable of gaining a high grade. Despite her own rather undistinguished educational record, Diana had always been keen that her sons should receive a top-flight education, study hard and go on to university.

Throughout her life, Diana had been highly embarrassed about her supposed lack of intelligence, frequently making jokes about her own limitations. In her heart, however, the fact that she never gained any 'O'-levels caused Diana much heart-ache and she didn't ever want either of her sons to feel inadequate in the way she had since she had left school at the age of 16.

Prince Charles explained to William that he was fortunate that he had been permitted to make his own decision to attend St Andrews rather than being advised — a polite word for ordered in royal circles — because in his days a variety of people had been involved in selecting the university where he was to study.

Indeed, William had to submit his request to attend St Andrews to those responsible for planning his life. These included not only Prince Charles but also the Queen, Prince

Philip, the Queen's Private Secretary, the Prime Minister and the Archbishop of Canterbury.

Prince Charles explained all this to William while he was still at Eton, emphasising that, as heir to the throne, his life would never be his own. He would have to learn to accept such decisions, and with good grace, because he was being groomed to be a future king. William didn't like to hear what his father was telling him but he knew that he had little choice but to accept the inevitable.

Following that conversation, William would tell his close pals at Eton that he now realised for the first time in his life what his mother had experienced in the years that she was a member of the Royal Family. William had all too often heard Diana complain in bitter terms about the orders she had to obey, handed down to her from some courtier or other who had been given the authority to tell Diana what she could and could not do. William knew such orders had frustrated and angered his mother, complaining that her life was no longer her own, unable to take decisions or please herself. The powers that be had demanded that everything she wanted to do had first to be cleared by them.

William talked to his father about the problem, explaining that he now understood what his mother had gone through. He understood why she kept complaining about being 'trapped' in Kensington Palace, only being allowed out when some faceless mandarin gave permission. William told his father that already he felt the same feelings and he asked whether the situation would get any better as he grew older. Charles answered him honestly, telling him that for the greater part of his life he had had to obey orders, always having to check with the officials if this, or that, would be permitted. Sometimes he had to argue with them when they made a decision that he couldn't accept.

Occasionally, Charles explained, but very infrequently, he would go to the ultimate authority — his mother — if he believed the mandarins were being unreasonable. And Charles explained that it wouldn't be so difficult for William because one day he,

Charles, would be the ultimate authority and he knew that the relationship between them was far closer than Charles' relationship had ever been with either of his parents. William left that meeting feeling much better because he trusted his father. He might have to go through a few tough years but eventually he believed his life would be far easier than his father's had ever been.

But William's education has now taken a different course from virtually any other young man in Britain. He has finished school and he will go to university somewhere. But he has far more to learn.

Like his father before him, William must learn everything about Britain and how the whole system actually works. William will learn how the nation is governed, how the government works, how affairs of state are conducted, how the armed services are run, how parliament works, how the City of London makes its money, how the law is applied and how the British justice system works.

And this knowledge William will have to learn at first hand. When the opportunity presents itself, William will visit various government offices and will be given conducted tours so that he can personally understand how the country works and how everything is run by the Civil Service which prides itself on centuries of tradition and excellence. His first stop will be Number 10 Downing Street, where he will have a meeting with the Prime Minister before setting off on his tour of numerous government offices. Among those offices will be the Foreign and Commonwealth Office and the Home Office, for example. At both, he will meet the ministers and, later, a senior civil servant will be detailed to give William a conducted tour of the offices explaining everything that is carried out and how the affairs of state are conducted.

He will spend a few days sitting in on government department meetings, some with ministers present, so that he will have an understanding of the interaction between ministers and civil servants. He will meet the staff and they, in turn, will explain to him exactly how their particular department works and what its responsibilities are. He will visit the Treasury to see how decisions are made about the imposition of taxes and how particular decisions are reached and the pros and cons of what effect any particular tax might have on the nation at large.

He will visit the Bank of England and the Stock Exchange, and the various London commodity markets trading in minerals, gold, silver, oil, coffee or whatever. He will see how the City is regulated and spend some time in one of the major British banks where he will learn how the money markets work across the world. He will probably also visit the Department of Health and the offices of the Department of Social Security. All these visits will be made over a period of a year or two and, ultimately, William will have a working knowledge of how the nation functions and how the various strands of government operate.

But in most of the serious conversations between father and son, Charles would continue to return to the one straightforward subject that would dominate William's entire life — duty. Charles would sometimes quote

George Eliot on his view of duty, 'God is inconceivable, immortality is unbelievable, but duty is peremptory and absolute.'

And Charles would explain to William that there could be no 'ifs and buts' in his life. He could never look the other way and pretend he hadn't heard for duty would have to come before all else, even his wife, his family and his children. If there was a clash of circumstances, he would have no option but to put duty first and the rest of his life would be of secondary importance. Charles explained that being a member of the Royal Family automatically entailed every member having a duty to the nation, but being the heir to the throne, and eventually the sovereign, would entail becoming a slave to duty. There was no other way.

Charles would tell him that he had no option but to understand and accept the fact, however unpalatable he found the prospect. And William would talk to his pals about the life that lay ahead of him but he showed no enthusiasm for the prospect. The problem was that William enjoyed life at Eton, particularly his final year when he was a prefect. Within reason, he had great freedom to do virtually whatever he wished. The senior pupils could go out together in Windsor, visit pubs or wine bars, spend weekends away from college, stay up chatting till ten at night and some of them did have girlfriends whom they would hope to see at weekends.

With Eton behind him, William also had to start training for the job that lay ahead. Professional speech-makers will advise William on how to behave when addressing an audience which will include basic instruction on how to stand, how to hold his hands, and how to capture and hold the attention of an audience of ten people or a thousand. He will spend hours learning how to deliver speeches, how to write them and how to inject interest and the odd touch of humour.

William was always very aware that his mother hated making speeches at any time. He knew that she would become nervous whenever she had to stand up and say a few words. On several occasions, Diana told William how she loathed the idea of standing up alone and making a speech because she felt vulnerable and worried that she might make a fool of herself. It hadn't helped her confidence when members of the Royal Family joked in private about her nervous speech-making, causing her to feel embarrassed and foolish. The idea of making a long speech so terrified Diana that she never said more than a few words, at the most speaking for only a few minutes. But William has more confidence. Eton has helped him to learn some skills in standing up and saying a few words and he is not fazed at the prospect of making speeches.

However, William will apparently need little or no instruction on how to hold one-to-one conversations with people. It seems that William learned that technique from his mother for he had watched her on numerous occasions chatting quietly to people sometimes in a hospital or clinic, an old people's home, be they a victim of an anti-personnel mine or of AIDS.

A palace courtier who has seen William talking on a one-to-one basis with a young drug addict said, 'He is a natural. It was simply unbelievable to see William chatting away, in a sympathetic way with the addict as though he understood everything the other teenager was going through. I thought of his mother immediately and it was uncanny how he won the confidence of the teenager in exactly the same way as Princess Diana won the confidence of strangers she spoke to. He will need no training in how to talk to people. It must be in the genes but I was really impressed at his ability to put people at their ease and give them confidence to speak to him about very personal matters. He is really very good.'

Throughout the next few years, during holidays from university, William is expected to spend time going out on official occasions with his father, accompanying him around the country, having the opportunity to see how such visits are organised and what he should do and not do at such times. It will also give people the opportunity to meet the young heir to the throne, to make their own judgements and assessments of William, his attitude and, to a certain extent, his character.

During his holidays from St Andrews it is

likely that William will accompany his father on official royal visits, particularly overseas to countries like Canada, Australia, New Zealand and other Commonwealth nations. Such visits would help to secure their continued support for having a member of the House of Windsor as their Head of State.

All members of the Royal Family and those who advise them know full well that Prince William is already being seen as the young man who will re-invigorate the Royal Family. There are others who would go further and believe the fate of the House of Windsor rests on his young shoulders. It is a huge responsibility, and one for which William has not yet been fully briefed.

William loves Canada. During his visit to Canada with his father and Harry in the spring of 1998, William learned to relax and really enjoy himself. He found Canadians, both men and women, young and old, easy to talk to and he related to them almost immediately. He felt they behaved naturally with him, with no hint of stuffiness or affectation intended to impress him. He liked that and felt an immediate rapport with the people. It seemed that the respect and friendliness was mutual for, when William flew back to London, he left behind a nation who had taken him to their hearts and not only because he was his mother's son.

As a result of that highly successful visit, which was only meant to be a skiing holiday with his father and Harry, the question of a far closer involvement between William and Canada has been discussed at the highest level in Buckingham Palace. Some courtiers believe that there might be a serious possibility of William becoming Governor-General of Canada in ten years' time. Some argued that William should not even be considered for the job before his thirtieth birthday because he would be too young, but there were others who argued that Canada was a young country whose people would probably love the idea of having such a youthful Governor-General as William.

The Royal Family has accepted that Australia is on the verge of establishing a republic and replacing the British sovereign as Head of State. Despite the fact that Australians voted in December 1999 against establishing a republic, there is a strong feeling that there may well be another referendum on the same matter within the next five years. The received wisdom is that at the next referendum the nation will vote for a republic. The Queen is known to have resigned herself to what she believes is the inevitable.

On the other hand, Canada is viewed differently because having the British monarch as official Head of State identifies the nation as totally separate from its all-powerful neighbour, the United States. Canadians are still proud to have the Queen as Head of State and if William's popularity continues among Canadians, there is a real possibility that one day William may become their Governor-General.

But the job William will one day undertake will not be a decision taken lightly. He may not yet even be aware that his job will not be his decision alone, but a decision taken in concert with a group of people. If he is fortunate, William will be permitted to discuss the affair and offer his opinion, but he will not necessarily be able to make the decision for himself.

Among those who will make that decision, whether to become Governor-General of Canada or whatever, will be senior royal courtiers who will sound out the rich and powerful in British society. Of course, the Queen will be heavily involved and, to a lesser extent, Prince Philip. Charles, of course, will have an important say in the matter. Others will include the Prime Minister of the day, the Archbishop of Canterbury, the Queen's Private Secretary and perhaps William's university tutor who will have been close to William over a three-year period.

Much will depend on the popularity and prestige of the Royal Family at the time that decision is taken. It may be that he will be required to undertake a heavy engagement of royal duties some time around the age of 25 which would mean he would be unable to have a career in the armed forces. That would not be popular with William but he might not have much of a choice.

There are a number of senior courtiers

who believe that William will be the young man on whom the House of Windsor comes to depend for its very survival. In the years immediately prior to the death of Diana, there were some courtiers who believed the Royal Family was facing a real crisis with the majority of the British people beginning to question whether the Britain of the twenty-first century needed a monarchy. The disillusionment had been caused by the marriage break-up of Charles and Diana and the controversy surrounding it. Many people believed that Diana had been harshly treated by the Royal Family and they strongly supported her in her struggle with the monarchy and Buckingham Palace officials.

Already, it is accepted among many courtiers that William could become the man whose presence will make or break the House of Windsor. If the young, handsome, charismatic and lovable young prince develops into a mature man who is respected by the population at large, then many believe the future of the House of Windsor will be safe. At present, no one is even contemplating what might happen otherwise because there is so much confidence in William and his natural ability to win friends. It may seem ironic that the very qualities that Diana brought to the marriage which proved so disastrous to the Royal Family may yet be responsible for her son saving the House of Windsor.

During his gap year and his years at St Andrews, William will live at both Highgrove and St James Palace. Most of William's Eton friends lived either in London or, like William, their parents had a house in London and another in the country. William is keen to make his main base in London and keep a bedroom for himself at Highgrove where he can stay at weekends.

Most of the girls he knows all live in London, or stay in London most of the time. And most dinner and drinks parties take place in London during the week.

In the same way as Diana loved the buzz of London, the *frisson* of London's restaurants, the fun and exhilaration of dinner parties and drinks parties, so does young William. As he tells his friends, there is nothing that he finds more exciting than going out to a restaurant with friends and not being recognised. He loves to be able to be himself, chat, crack jokes and talk to girls with only those at his table knowing his real identity. Occasionally, he can still manage to go unrecognised but those occasions are becoming more rare and he doesn't like it.

As with most young men, William loves sport and enjoys it. Whatever he does once his full-time education has been completed, he intends to go on participating in sport for as long as possible. He told his father that he would like to be able to use Chelsea Harbour or one of the other exclusive London sports clubs for swimming and tennis. He is also thinking seriously of joining one of the Thames rowing clubs, like Leander. The Eton master in charge of rowing believes that William could become a champion oarsman if he was given proper professional training because of the great potential he showed in competitions at Eton. But the master explained to William that to achieve competition standard in the real world would take a great deal of hard work and dedication. He had no doubt, however, that William had the natural ability to succeed. He believed it would depend on William's commitment to the sport as to what standard of competition he would achieve.

Like his father and his paternal grandfather before him, William has already caught the polo bug. During the summer of 1999, he began taking polo lessons with a member of his father's old club, The Guards Polo Club at Windsor Great Park. William is a competent rider and, as a result, he picked up the rudiments of the game quite easily. He also has a good eye which is an important element in the sport. During this summer, William also took further lessons and he practices stick-and-ball at Highgrove under the watchful eye of Prince Charles. Not to be outdone by his elder brother, the adventurous, hard-riding Harry has also taken up the sport and is determined to achieve a higher standard than his father.

Like Charles before him, William will soon be seen taking part in practice chukkas and then competitive matches and before long it is expected that he will be making regular appearances at Windsor Great Park. Those who run the Guards polo club believe the arrival of Prince William on the polo scene will bring an increased interest in the sport, and not only among polo players and lovers of the sport. Many who attended polo at Windsor during Charles's bachelor days recall the occasions when he would arrive at the ground in his dark blue Aston Martin convertible accompanied by a mystery girlfriend. It was at polo that Charles was first seen with the teenage Diana. As the late Susie Barrantes, Sarah Ferguson's beloved mother, once said: 'Doesn't everyone meet on the polo field?'

And then there is William's new passion — shooting. He spent many weekends during last winter on shoots all over Britain.

And then there is the question of finance. If William decides to join the armed forces, he will of course draw the pay for the job as his father did during his years in the Royal Navy. But an heir to the throne cannot live on that level of income.

William will need his own staff, though not

when he attends university. During the time he is at university he will, of course, need two full-time bodyguards with other members of the Royal Protection Squad standing by for holidays and occasions when he might be meeting members of the public. Until he begins to undertake official royal duties, he will receive no income from the Queen or the Civil List. In this interim period, he will receive an income each month from his father. He will also continue to have use of an American Express card and the monthly account, as now, will be paid by Charles. Other expenditure, such as William's clothes, shoes and sports equipment are also met by Prince Charles.

Since Tiggy Legge-Bourke married and left royal employment at the end of 1999, Ruth Clarke has joined the Princes of Wales's office to take care of both William's and Harry's affairs. Her relationship with both William and Harry is, however, far different from the close personal relationship both teenagers enjoyed with Tiggy. In fact, Ruth Clarke rarely leaves the office and only sees the princes infrequently. She is responsible for looking after their diaries, checking school dates, important occasions, holidays and the weekends they will spend with their father, other members of the Royal Family or friends. She replies to letters on their behalf and accepts suitable invitations.

Thus far, Ruth Clarke's duties have been manageable but as soon as William embarks on university education, keeping track of his various invitations and appointments, his sporting activities and his social life will become a far more complicated affair. One of her tasks will be to know Prince William's whereabouts at any given moment, which is likely to prove a difficult task given the freedom he loves and yearns for. But he will need no other staff until he begins undertaking official royal duties.

Now William is 19 and a new life opens before him. He is fully aware that as heir to the throne his life will be dictated by duty and by the demands and expectations of the nation. He has no illusions about the demands that duty will place upon him. But he is also determined to try and enjoy life to the full, particularly on the sporting front. William knows that he will have to balance his duty to the nation and the Royal Family with his own wishes and his own character. But of one thing he is positive. He has never forgotten the words his mother would say to him as he was growing up — 'Be your own man.' Come what may, William is determined to be his own man.